THE
WILD
SIDE OF TOWN

CHRIS BAINES

BBC PUBLICATIONS AND
ELM TREE BOOKS · LONDON

ACKNOWLEDGMENTS

Robber-Barons past and present! They are the people I owe a note of thanks to. Without their greedy exploitation of the land in the industrial towns of the last century, our urban wildspace simply wouldn't exist. They created the quarries, canals, railway cuttings, waste tips and dereliction which is now so rich in wild plants and animals.

They're still at work today, too. Their short-sighted industrialisation of the countryside has driven wildlife into town, and alerted you and me to the conservation crisis. Even the present terrible levels of high unemployment have a silver lining. Thousands of young, enthusiastic, idealistic people, robbed of permanent jobs, have turned their energies towards the urban landscape. Their input into organisations such as the Urban Wildlife Group, Landlife, The Avon and London Wildlife Trusts, and the Conservation Volunteers is a constant source of inspiration and encouragement to me.

I hope in return, that this book does their work justice, and that it will help persuade everyone that 'helping people and wildlife to get together in towns' is a valuable way to provide many more folk with *permanent*, generously paid jobs.

CHRIS BAINES,
HAGLEY, MAY 1986

The author and publishers would like to thank the following for permission to use copyright photographs:

Heather Angel/Biofotos p. 64 (photo by Karl Holgård); Ardea p. 28 (photo by David and Katie Urry), p. 45 (photo by John Daniels), p. 72 (photo by John Mason); BBC Publications/Nigel Bradley front cover; Bruce Coleman Ltd title page (photo by R. Wilmshurst), p. 60, p. 69 (photos by Kim Taylor); Eric and David Hosking p. 24 (photo by John Hawkins); Frank Lane Picture Agency p. 21 (photo by A. R. Hamblin); London Wildlife Trust opposite p. 1; NHPA p. 29 (photo by David Woodfall), p. 32 (photo by L. Campbell); Hugh Oliffe p. 4 top, p. 5; Radio Times/Richard Farley back cover; Saxon Wildlife Films front cover inset, opposite title page, p. 33 (photos by Mike Leach); Neys Jones (p. 4 bottom). All other photographs by the author. Diagrams by Stephen Lings and Brian Watson/Linden Artists.

First published in Great Britain in 1986
by Elm Tree Books/Hamish Hamilton Ltd
27 Wrights Lane London W8 5TZ

and

BBC Publications, a division of BBC Enterprises Ltd
35 Marylebone High Street London W1M 4AA

© 1986 by J. Christopher Baines

ISBN 0 241 11995 2 (Elm Tree)/0 563 21312 4 (BBC)
0 241 11942 1 (Elm Tree)/0 563 21309 4 (BBC) pbk

Published to accompany a series of programmes
prepared in consultation with the BBC
Continuing Education Advisory Council

Set in 11/13 pt Ehrhardt by Rowland Phototypesetting Ltd,
Bury St Edmunds, Suffolk.

Printed in Italy by AGV, Vicenza, Mondadori Group

CONTENTS

GROWING UP

1

Where did you play when you were little? Where was your favourite landscape? I don't mean your first choice for a day out. I mean the special, magical, secret place you visited every day; the spot where you built your dens, had your tea parties, counted your conkers and picked your nosegays.

Throughout my life, my own special childhood landscape has quietly continued to influence all my feelings about nature, the seasons and many other things besides. At the time, though, it was just a great place for adventure. Of course it wasn't one single place. It was a network of green,

Children choose to play in wild, unofficial landscapes, and can't avoid contact with nature. Why do grown ups dismiss these landscapes simply as 'untidy'?

all within about five hundred yards of home – more or less within yelling distance at bedtime. Looking back, one of the most interesting things about it is the fact that all of it was 'unofficial', and most of it was wild. When I was very little, my adventures were restricted to the garden, but even then it was the secret, squeeze-into space at the back of the shed that held most delights. Once I was allowed out, I quickly established a territory and this had various highspots. There was my dark, damp hiding place amongst the huge wooden barrels of the vinegar factory – making the smell of malt vinegar unquestionably the most powerful memory-jerker of all for me. There was Mr Brundell's wonderful abandoned garden, complete with a jungle of raspberry canes, huge forests of rhubarb, great bushes of sweet-smelling lilac, oceans of stinging nettles, and fortunately, lots of antidotal dock leaves. I had a five-star den here. It was a shallow hole amongst the raspberries, covered with a sheet of corrugated iron, and camouflaged with dead grass. In time, my friend and I furnished it with a carpet, and it always had a jam-jar of flowers for decoration.

The most exciting, and certainly the most forbidden part of my territory was 'the quarry'. The rock was soft sandstone, dynamited out in great avalanches, crushed in a giant, noisy tin-clad machine and carted away in a stream of big, dripping-wet lorries which seemed to bounce endlessly backwards and forwards along the access road. Everything in and around that quarry was covered in bright golden-yellow sand, stuck together with even yellower clay. This mixture covered the buildings, the roads, the lorries, and a good deal of the time it covered me, too. The floor of the quarry was low in one corner, and the real fascination of the place lay in the pond of shallow water which collected there. The water was crystal clear, but one good swirl with a stick, or more probably a piece of old pram handle, and the yellow mixture of clay and silt would cloud the view. I spent hours stirring it up and watching it clear again.

Mine wasn't a deep, sinister quarry. The colour of the rock made it seem permanently sunny, and that pond always offered some new experience. This was the place where I found my first dead dragonfly – huge and green and shiny. It was the source of an endless supply of tadpoles and sticklebacks, and inevitably, it was the place where I first felt the unforgettable sensation of icy cold water trickling over the top of my wellington boots.

The one other vitally important landscape of my formative years was 'the hills and mountains'. This was a patch of tipped land, covered in piles of soil and demolition rubble, and clothed in wild grasses, brambles, and the odd patch of garden throw-outs. I remember being thrilled to find a patch of purple crocuses flowering there once, obviously the contents of a plant pot abandoned the year before. Were these really wild crocuses? Of course they were – and very rare. Although even my podgy seven-year-old legs could run the full length of the hills and mountains in about three minutes, the detour often added half an hour to the journey home.

The thing that made this landscape so fascinating was the variety of junk that people dumped there. Mostly this consisted of such invaluable items as pram chassis – ideal for trolley-making; huge Bakelite radio sets – full of valves and covered in knobs ripe for the picking; empty Tizer bottles that represented money back and a private income – but only if they still had their gritty black screw-top intact. The find of the century, I remember, was a huge heap of tins each containing hundreds of penny-chew toffee bars. We'd been learning about South America at the time, and the Spanish search for El Dorado. Suddenly I could identify with the conquistadors, though I never actually dared eat my sticky gold – it was blighted by gang-chatter about "poisoned toffee" and stolen goods. That must have been the most fingered and least sucked toffee in history.

Thinking back, it is not too fanciful to imagine that this daytime territory of mine was equally familiar to our local fox. I do remember finding a perfectly straight line of his tracks in the snow on the back lawn one winter. No doubt he dropped in quite often for a late night drink at the quarry pond, and a midnight feast of frogs if they were on the menu. The hills and mountains must have yielded a steady supply of voles and beetles from the depths of the long grass, and certainly he would have had no pangs of conscience about eating stolen chew-bars.

With so much wild and varied landscape to play in, I must have been constantly surrounded by nature, but I was hardly ever conscious of it as anything other than a wild setting for adventures. Certainly I never did anything as earnest as identifying wildflowers, or serious bird-watching, and I can't remember anyone who did. I do remember being lifted up to see into the nest of a hedge sparrow once, and watching in disbelief as a whole family of weasels flowed along the

The unacceptable face of 'municipal recreational provision'. The swings have actually been removed, to avoid danger – so the kids tightrope walk along the top instead. We can find cash to re-tarmac redundant play-areas, but not to employ playleaders to work in the wildspace.

Is it fly-tipping – or an airline pilot's driving seat? This is the land of dens, and secret adventures. The rubbish adults dump is instantly adopted by local kids.

bottom of the stone wall in the front garden, but these were the exceptions that proved the rule. Nature was not a serious issue. It was just a general part of the landscape, and that is the way it is for almost everyone. That magical familiarity is so easily killed by the kindness of an adult preoccupation with naming things, collecting things and explaining things. The most important thing of all is that nature, wildlife, should be such a familiar part of our surroundings that we can relax, and take it for granted simply as part of being outside.

For all my apparent lack of serious interest in natural history, it is remarkable, and reassuring, to remember just how strongly the patterns of my life were, and still are, linked to the natural calendar. The year seemed always to begin and end with me standing wide-eyed beneath a street lamp, catching snowflakes in my gaping mouth, hypnotised by their endless stream, oblivious to the cold, and escaping from the pressures of choir practice. In March the world revolved around frogspawn, and then the inevitable jars full of 'taddies'. Coltsfoot flowers were always the first of the year to be picked and taken home, and then the bird-nesting season was in full swing. It is difficult, from an adult perspective, to

Tadpoles are for sharing. By getting involved with environmental education, I get the chance to relive my own childhood.

excuse the damage I must have done in my quest for the eggs of common birds. The craze only lasted a couple of seasons (thank goodness), but I must admit that, unpalatable though it may seem now, I learned a great deal about wildlife, and habitat, and I read a good deal too, thanks to that barbaric hobby. I certainly learned how vicious hawthorn can be, and how effectively magpies protect their nests with baskets of thorns. I am quite sure that if the Young Ornithologists Club had existed then, I would have been an early convert, and could have been shown how to enjoy the pleasure without the plunder.

The wild plant which featured most strongly in my landscape was the elder. Its characteristic smell is still every bit as evocative as the vinegar. Of course mine wasn't the first generation to find the elder had magical properties, but my version was a little less orthodox than the druids'. I think elder commanded a basic respect in me from a very early age, because no matter how often Dad chopped down the one at the side of the house, it just leapt back to life, and grew even more vigorously. Even now, thirty or more years later, it still yields enough fruit for a couple of gallons of wine each season. I had one or two particularly big elderberry bushes in my territory that were OK for climbing and had just the right amount of brittleness to make the exercise risky. Their umbrella-like habit makes them the ideal summer den habitat, of course, and the flowers and fruit are very special. Elder flowers really are wonderful. They smell delicious, are perfect in their detail, and attract lots of tiny little black insects to their

Coltsfoot – a tough urban wildflower which thrives in the poorest of conditions. Any child will see it as a precious, pretty wildflower – until someone explains that it's 'a weed'.

nectar. They can be harvested and turned into elderflower champagne, or if left intact, they develop first into hard green pellets, ideal ammunition for peashooters, and into the purple berries which stain tongue, fingers and clothes, and taste (almost) too bitter to eat.

If I add in the conker harvest, blackberry picking, collecting the dead wood for bonfire night, and the fun of kicking up autumn leaves, then it is quite clear that I had very close links with nature, but the idea of being 'a naturalist' never even crossed my mind.

If any of these personal memories of mine ring a bell with you, then I hope you are beginning to see why wildlife in towns is so important. Everyone needs contact with nature. At the age of eight or nine it happens without question, and even in adulthood, the vast majority of people prefer green surroundings to the drabness of concrete and tarmac, but somehow as we grow up, wildness is re-labelled untidiness, and although we still prefer to walk the dog along the overgrown canalside, rather than the neatly manicured park path, there is a resistance to the idea that wildlife can be an acceptable part of city living. Millions of people feed the birds in their garden each winter, but they also complain when the council fails to mow the road verge, and they spray their roses with chemicals rather than tolerate the caterpillars which mean so much to the birds they helped to overwinter.

There is a real danger that the grown-up world could lose touch with nature completely. In this book I hope I can remind you of some of the pleasure wildlife can bring. More importantly, I want to show you that there is no need to become a 'committed conservationist' or move to the depths of the countryside in order to enjoy nature.

We all feel better when we have contact with living things. Our towns and cities are full of wonderful wildlife and I can show you where to find it. Once you have discovered your local hedgehogs, foxes, dragonflies and kestrels, I hope you will use this book to help protect their habitats. Use it, too, to persuade local councillors, parks managers and your overtidy neighbours to create new places for wildlife, as well as taking better care of those which are already there.

Wildlife in towns is something everyone can enjoy, but it does need help and protection, and you are obviously an ideal person to take on some of that pleasant responsibility.

THE RURAL MYTH

2

There is a popular myth that British wildlife still lives exclusively in the countryside, and is to be enjoyed only by the tweedy squirearchy, or strange people called naturalists, who wear woolly bobblehats, coats made of tarpaulin, and always have a pair of 'bins' round their necks. Until very recently, all of that would have been true, but it certainly isn't an accurate picture any longer. Natural history may still be the remote, slightly eccentric specialism it always was, but a love of British wildlife is something quite different. In the past ten years, we have seen an avalanche of wildlife programmes on radio and TV, with audiences for *The World About Us* and *The Natural World* regularly topping those for *Match of the Day*. All of the voluntary conservation organisations have experienced a spectacular growth in membership too, yet I suspect relatively few of their followers would describe themselves as 'naturalists'. They just want to help birds, or they think hedgehogs, frogs and butterflies are important. A basic love of nature is something which the vast majority of people share, and the important thing to realise is that ordinary people are no longer embarrassed about admitting it. After all, if a big, butch male like David Bellamy can enthuse about buttercups and daisies, so can everyone else.

The other spectacular change that has taken place in the past forty years or so is the scale of wildlife habitat loss. It is true, of course, that our landscape has suffered some spectacular shocks in the past. When the last Ice Age retreated, about 8000 years ago, the seas rose, and we were cut adrift from the mainland of Europe, the rubble and debris left by the ice were quickly colonised by the wind-borne seed of pioneer plants. As the climate improved, the landscape was clothed in woodland, with just a few gaps where ground was unstable, or mountain tops were too bleak. We still have small fragments of that primary woodland around, even today. Parts of Sherwood and Epping Forests are quite large examples, and there are smaller pockets in most counties. These are our most ancient habitats – undoubtedly the most precious of all our landscape features. Even so, we continue to chop them down and grub them up to make way for motorways, housing estates and supermarkets.

The vast majority of that primary woodland was lost long ago. In fact, most of it had been cleared by our first generations of speculative developers – those pioneering people who tired of the hunter-gatherer way of life, and cleared the forest for firewood and for farming. That first big change started around 5000 years ago, and we had lost most of our forest by the time the Romans turned up. Of course clearance then was a relatively slow business. There is a world of difference between a stone axe and a JCB. As the woodland made way for pasture, and then arable fields, other species of both plants and animals which would have been very rare in the forest became more and more common. Obviously the grasses and the meadow wildflowers began to have a field day, and along with them came the meadow butterflies, the skylarks and the grasshoppers. Some woodland species adapted. No doubt the mole enjoyed its new grassland territory, and the relative abundance of earthworms, even if the digging was more difficult than it used to be in soft leafmould, and the molehills more obvious to predators. Plants such as the groundsel and the cornflower would have been extremely rare in both the forest and the grassland. They are annuals which need to shed their seed on to disturbed soil, and so they would have been restricted to the odd collapsed river bank, the top of a

Some of our countryside still looks wonderful – but the combination of big machines and chemicals means such beauty is skin deep.

molehill, or the soil exposed by the up-turned roots of a fallen tree. Herds of wild pigs would have done a bit of grubbing around, of course, and opened up the soil in forest clearings. The robin, nowadays one of our most familiar birds, appears like magic at the mere suggestion of a bit of digging. In the primeval forest robins would probably have confined their activities to pecking around the foraging swine.

Once man began to cultivate the land and grow crops, these previously rare opportunists would have boomed. In no time at all, a plague of groundsel, chickweed, sowthistle, dandelion and all those other weeds of the veg patch must have swept across Britain, revelling in the massive expanse of freshly disturbed ground. With these weeds, the flocks of seed-eating birds, and the insects that eat their leaves and pollinate their colourful flowers would soon have followed. All this wildlife that depends on cultivation has been a feature of our landscape now for more than a thousand years.

There was another great upheaval in the countryside a couple of hundred years ago. The landscape, which had been blown open by forest clearance, cultivated by the common people in huge communal fields, criss-crossed with occasional boundary hedges and ditches, and sprinkled with marshes and relics of woodland – that 'champion landscape' was suddenly and dramatically chopped into bits. The patchwork of tiny fields, and the thousands of miles of enclosing hedgerow that divided them, were created in just a few decades. The Enclosures Acts led to commonland being parcelled up as individual farms for the first time. As our familiar picturebook landscape took shape, to the horror of

This may be a great achievement in terms of agricultural productivity, but it has been achieved at vast public expense, through extraordinarily inefficient use of energy. Very few wild plants or animals can live in wall-to-wall winter wheat.

environmental commentators of the day, there was the
knock-on effect of a massive drift of people from the countryside
to the industrial towns and cities.

With such a history of changing fortunes, it is tempting to
believe the propaganda which suggests that the agricultural
revolution of the past forty years is just another turn of the
screw – that the wildlife will adapt. Certainly the physical
changes to the patchwork landscape are no greater in scale
than those of the enclosures that created it. This time,
though, there is the secret ingredient of chemical warfare, and
we are dealing with the last straw so far as many of our
ancient and precious landscape features are concerned.

The loss of any of our tiny remnants of primary woodland
is total, absolute and in no way compensated for by any
amount of new planting. An ecological community of plants
and animals which has taken seven or eight thousand years
to develop is incredibly complex. The relationships between
the various species are tightly interwoven, and cannot
possibly be re-created in a new patch of planting. Since 1947
we have destroyed 40% of the small relics which had hung
on since the Ice Age.

Hay meadows had been a part of our landscape and our
culture for a thousand years. Where would Constable, or
even Laurie Lee, have been without them? Those magical
meadows have been almost totally wiped out since the war. Of
all the acres that were there when I was born, just 3% still
survive, to show us how beautiful cowslips, fritillaries and
yellow rattle used to be. Not all those mourned-for meadows
have been ploughed up or built on, either. Many of them
are still green. In fact they're rather too green. This is where
chemical warfare is so devastating. The process of feeding
with bags of artificial fertilisers and spraying with selective
chemicals is 'modern farming technique'. Its aim is to make the
grass grow stronger, but in the process all the wildflowers
disappear and when they have gone, no amount of
conscience-caring will bring them back. The political origin
of this 'maximum productivity' agriculture was a wish to
become self-sufficient after the blockades of the Second
World War. The irony is that high input-high output farming
depends largely on imported chemical fertiliser and raw
materials, so a blockade would still leave us hungry.

The picture is just as gloomy with wetlands. Digging a ditch
used to be a hard, wet, miserable job. No one would tackle
the task joyously. Now, of course, we have machines that allow

ditches to be dug from the relative comfort of a cosy cab. It
is quicker, neater and, with huge grants of public money as
an incentive, it is not surprising that our wetlands, our boggy
fields, marshes and fens have been drained relentlessly to
produce yet more high-productivity farmland. All too often
the soil from the ditch has been used to fill in an inconvenient
nearby pond – thus killing at least two birds with one stone.
In fact, this drainage mania has had significant international
impact. Britain is of great importance as a terminus for
millions of migrant ducks, geese and other wetland birds. As
we've dried out their traditional wintering grounds,
populations have plummeted. Fifty per cent of our lowland
marshes have been drained in forty years, and wetland
wildlife is now at an all-time low, with once common species
such as teal, snipe and redshank becoming increasingly rare.
Even animals as familiar as the common frog and the smooth
newt have dropped in numbers by as much as 90% in ten
years in many agricultural areas. A child in the countryside is
hard pressed to find tadpoles to catch these days.

Simple loss of habitat is bad enough, but again there is a
chemical sting in the tail. Those ditches, streams and ponds
that do manage to survive are becoming heavily polluted as
more and more inorganic chemicals are scattered over the
land. Nitrates leach through the soil into the land drains, and
in no time at all the ditches and streams are clogged with
blanket weed which cuts out the light, and causes even more
severe problems when it dies, sinks to the bottom, and
becomes a decaying sludge. In the summer of 1985 I filmed
on the River Perry in Shropshire. This was chosen as an
excellent example of a wildlife-rich, relatively clean rural river.
Six weeks later it was dead from end to end – killed by a
tidal wave of poisonous slurry released mistakenly and illegally
from an intensive pig farm, deep in the heart of the tranquil,
cosy 'caring' countryside.

So much doom and gloom is depressing, so it's hardly
surprising that people choose not to see the scale of the
damage. Certainly the spread of Dutch Elm disease, with its
denuding effect on the Midlands in particular, has had much
more impact on the public than the pollution of streams, or
the degrading of our meadows. Even that 'act of God' was
perpetrated by human incompetence, when diseased logs were
imported from North America with their bark intact – but
in a way the evil little elm bark beetle, and its deadly partner
in crime, the super-effective fungus, did the countryside a

Familiar?
Upper Slaughter, in the
Cotswolds, is one of the three or
four countryside cliches the TV and
film producers depend on. There
are precious few 'unspoiled
corners' left.

great service. The change it produced in the space of just two
or three years reminded all of us that the countryside was
vulnerable, and when we looked a little closer, we discovered
that there was more than just quantitative damage. Not only
were we losing half our hedgerows, and much of our ancient
woodland, but the *quality* of the landscape which remained
was being very seriously and irreversibly damaged. Modern
chemical farming with its brutal machines and its subsidised
monocultures was sterilising the landscape. A rich farming
countryside, full of wildlife and history, was already largely
a thing of the past.

Our green, rich, beautiful landscape is arguably our greatest
single currency earner. As well as exporting millions of
dollars worth of greenery in the hearts, minds and cameras of
foreign visitors, we feature it in our films and TV
programmes, in the reprints of Constable's *Haywain*, in our
literature and in a thousand more subtle ways. Amazing,
then, that we should have spent so much of that income
subsidising the killing of the goose that lays the golden eggs. Of
course, one of the problems is that you can still find a pretty
bit to photograph. The Countryside Commission can still
manage to string together a blossom route for the grockles,
and so the myth is sustained. There is, however, a limit to
the ingenuity of even the most talented public relations officer
or film director. Have you noticed recently that every rural
period drama, from Saxon to Victorian times, seems to have
taken place in either Upper Slaughter or Shaftesbury? In
fact, even those locations are getting a bit threadbare, and
future celluloid glimpses of the dreamlike English
countryside seem likely to be 'made in France'.

HOW MUCH WILDLIFE REALLY LIVES IN TOWNS?

3

At first glance, towns and cities seem to be made up entirely of buildings and tarmac. In fact, there are masses of green open spaces in even the most urban of cities. Travel by train instead of road, and you begin to get some idea of the space that lies behind the street scene. Travel through a city like Birmingham, along its peaceful canals, and the wild greenness of the place is almost unbelievable. The spaces are getting bigger too, as more and more factories close, and the few surviving industries move to motorway junctions in the countryside or green field sites on the edge of town.

As you sit on your suburban train, rattling in from commuter land, or out to holiday land, the first thing you should notice is that your railway line is running through a green corridor of leafy embankments, rocky cuttings and neglected, wild railway land. This corridor, and the many others like it, are vital to the wildlife living in towns. They play the same role that the much lamented hedgerows used to play in the countryside. They provide habitats in themselves, but perhaps more importantly, they enable wildlife to move around amongst the buildings, free from motor traffic and surprisingly free from human disturbance too. The railway corridors are easy to find, and they exist in almost every town and city. They link out into the countryside, and have no doubt provided an easy route from the pressures there for plants and animals alike. In the good old days of steam, there were frequent fires on the railway embankments, burning off the trees and shrubs and allowing the light in. I'm sure no one thought of those glowing sparks from the firebox as a habitat management tool, but there is no doubt that this

Old canals are like long, narrow, unpolluted lakes – the perfect way for dragonflies and kingfishers to move around the town.

casual burning helped improve the railway corridors for certain species. In letting the sunlight through to ground level it had an effect similar to that of the coppicing cycle in ancient woodland, and would encourage light-demanding flowers such as primroses, red campion, and foxgloves to bloom. You do still find these pretty wildflowers on railway banks, but they are much less common than they once were.

The operational railway lines, the ones Dr Beeching left behind, are particularly important as sanctuary land. Although the fencing may not always be perfect, people do tend to keep away from the lines that still have trains thundering along them. This lack of human disturbance makes them attractive to the more timid animals. There must be tens of thousands of urban foxes with their dens in the bramble-covered embankments of the inter-city lines. Increasingly, there are reports of badgers establishing setts here for the same reason. These banks of bramble that have become such a feature of our now unburned railway land are important to birds too. They provide nesting sites for many of the blackbirds, hedge sparrows and finches we see in our gardens, as well as secretive species such as the whitethroat and the linnet.

Many plants derive a special benefit from working railway corridors too. Although the parent plants obviously don't pick up their roots and scamper along the track at dead of night, they are able to move, nevertheless. Generation by generation, the species with wind-borne seed are sucked backwards and forwards along the corridors, swept along in the slipstream of passing trains. The most celebrated example of this hobo-lifestyle is a pretty weed called the Oxford ragwort. This plant was collected from its native habitat amongst the lava ash on the slopes of Mount Etna, in the middle of the last century, and lovingly brought back to grow in the collection at the Oxford Botanical Gardens. This botanical rarity, with its little yellow daisy-flowers, had the same bad habit as so many of its close relations: it produces masses of fluffy, parachute-carrying seed. In no time at all some of these had floated over the wall, and found the ideal lava-flow substitute in the ash and ballast of the local railway embankment. Once it had made its escape from the Botanical Gardens, the ragwort spread, generation by generation, along the railway network, through the Oxfordshire countryside, and into towns and villages all over Britain. Now it can be found growing on rubbly, lava-like wasteland everywhere.

Baby spiders, or spiderlings as they are called, also hitch a
ride in the slipstream in much the same way. They produce
a long thread of gossamer which acts like a miniature kite.
When a gust of wind catches it, the spiderling is whisked
off up into the pale blue yonder, sometimes travelling across
whole oceans before it touches ground again. The draught
caused by a passing train is more than enough to suck up a
spiderling and deposit it gently at the next station.

Road traffic creates a slipstream, too. No doubt this is the
way that famous rare spider *Tegenaria agrestis* managed to travel
from its only previously recorded site, somewhere in the New
Forest, to take up residence beneath the concrete columns
of Spaghetti Junction, 150 miles north.

Roads form another important part of the corridor network.
Most people are familiar with the kestrels that wind-hover
motionless over the long grass of the motorway embankments,
or sit on the top of road signs, their heads bobbing
menacingly in anticipation of a crashing dive and another furry
beakful. In Bangor, North Wales, there are frequent reports
of spectacular and very rare red kites doing much the same
thing, scavenging along the road verges, picking up carrion
as they used to do in smelly medieval streets. Talk about
keeping up with the Jones's! This could be the basis of a
whole new Twitcher Tourism industry. The rank, unkempt
grassy banks are a marvellous habitat for wildlife, and there is
now some evidence that the high nitrogen content of car
exhausts is actually boosting the growth of some of the
wildflowers, and that this in turn is producing higher than
average populations of insects. Any motorist knows that
motorway wildlife is thriving, simply from the number of red
and yellow splatmarks on the windscreen, and, of course,
the huge number of animals, both large and small, which we
see squashed on the roads each year. All these casualties
provide rich pickings for the carrion-eaters. You may not be
lucky enough to see red kites pecking away at the hedgehogs,
rabbits and other road victims, but you must have seen magpies
and crows cleaning up the remains, and daringly playing
chicken with the traffic.

Streams and rivers mesh into the wildlife network too.
Waterpower was an important base for much of our early
industry, and river transport was vital, too. As a result, many
of our towns and cities were founded along the riverbanks,
and were often clustered around easy crossing places. The
difficulty of building right by the river, combined with the

recent redundancy of much of the early development, means that there is often a substantial amount of wet, wild backland along these particular corridors, and this provides a migration route for water voles, kingfishers, dragonflies and a whole host of other water-based wildlife. The piles of flood-borne debris contain a ready supply of food for wild creatures, and the flowing water itself is a marvellous vehicle for both plants and animals. Any watercourse is very vulnerable, both to chemical pollution and to physical damage, but in recent years urban streams and rivers have benefited from the tightening of pollution controls, and since the drainage boards have been dominated and manipulated by influential farming landowners, all the worst destruction of the drainage engineers has been confined to the wetland and rivers of the countryside. There are signs now that both these aspects of urban river management are worsening fast, but more of that in chapter nine.

One more major wildlife corridor type deserves a special mention. The canal system of Britain had a brief but glorious history. It was eclipsed as a serious form of transport when the railways came along. The canals themselves still survive, however, and where they travel through towns they provide perhaps the best wildlife corridor of all. All wildlife needs water to survive, but many species have a particular and intimate relationship with it. Canals are like huge, long, narrow ponds. They are a still, gentle habitat, and where there is little disturbance, and no chemical pollution, they rapidly become spectacular havens for wildlife. All the beautiful waterside wildflowers of the ponds and lakes grow happily in the silt along the canalside. Moorhens and coots chug silently from bank to bank, nesting amongst the flag iris, and feeding amongst the rotting stems. There are damselflies, darting backwards and forwards just an inch or two above the water, and huge 'helicopter' dragonflies quartering the canal, then shooting off to snap up a midge or a butterfly over a nearby bramble patch. The towpath is an obvious traffic-free route for foxes. Kingfishers are moving further into town, hunting along the fish-rich canals, and the combination of tranquil, reflective water, freedom from road traffic, and wild vegetation really does bring the idealised dream countryside deep into the heart of the city.

This wonderful network of green corridors obviously allows the wildlife to move around easily and safely, but there is much more to the wildlife resource than railways, canals,

Road verges are just one of several kinds of wildlife corridors in towns. Unsprayed and undisturbed, they are becoming more and more rich in wildlife.

rivers and road verges. Each corridor is like a string of pearls, connecting together huge numbers of green spaces of all shapes and sizes. Some of them are tangled, wild and marvellous for wildlife just as they stand, whilst others are tidier but offer room for improvement. Collectively they represent perhaps 20% of even the most urban city. The Metropolitan West Midlands, for instance, has over 80,000 acres of unbuilt land, and well over a quarter of that area is wild, green, and considered to be of direct value to wildlife. That 20,000 acres, believe it or not, is 12% of the county area – a much higher proportion of wildscape than you could find on a modern farm.

Once you begin to consider the green side of the city, you will inevitably think of the parks and public open spaces – the official landscape. If you add in the school playingfields, the hospital lawns, the odd university or polytechnic campus, traffic islands and the land around housing estates, you can begin to see that there is a lot of land involved. Sadly, it is of very little value to wildlife, since the vast majority of it is maintained as close-mown grassland, with just the occasional forlorn lollipop tree for punctuation. We spend well over a thousand million pounds each year mowing the municipal grasslands of Britain. That is an awful lot of public money to pour into suppressing nature, but that is what it amounts to. Of course there is a place for neat, mown grass, and much of it is needed for football, hockey and other formal sports, but it really is a desert so far as wildlife is concerned. One of the few species to benefit from all this 'green concrete' is the starling. A hundred and fifty years ago these handsome birds were really very unusual, but they feed by probing their sharp beaks down amongst the grass roots and tugging out juicy leatherjackets. Close-mown grass is their ideal feeding ground, and so their numbers have soared. You can see them marching, head down, in big crowds, working their way relentlessly across the grasslands, generally under the bemused eye of a bored-looking black-headed gull. In fact, so attractive is our city parkland that an estimated thirty million starlings migrate here from the eastern bloc countries every winter.

The official open spaces may be hostile, windswept, close-mown and favoured by very few species. Fortunately there is an enormous amount of unofficial open space in towns to compensate. It is to these particular 'pearls' that the urban fox or the suburban badger will travel in search of food and shelter. Collectively, this might be described as urban wildspace, but it comes in many different forms, and each has a part to play.

Probably the most important, at least in conservation terms, are the very new sites and the very old ones. Taking the old ones first, I think it is fair to say that our industrial forefathers did a pretty haphazard job of expanding the towns. In the rush to build houses and factories, roads and railways, a great many bits of land got left behind – surrounded and swallowed up by the expanding urban sprawl. Sometimes the obstacle to development was landownership; some cantankerous old squire who refused to see his ancestral home turned over to rows of Coronation Street back-to-backs. These once rich country estates now form an important part of our official openspace network, and they do sometimes contain parkland trees, for instance, that pre-date the industrial revolution.

The most interesting of these relics, from the wildlife point of view, are the pockets of land that were passed over because they were too steep, or wet, or wooded to build in. These really are precious bits of ancient landscape and they often support fragments of their original wildlife population that have somehow clung on through two hundred years of life with noisy, dirty, town neighbours. The relics which are easy to spot are the woodlands, of course. There may be no more than half a dozen big, stag-headed senile oaks left now to break the skyline, but quite often you can find bluebells, yellow archangel, violet and wood anemone growing in the leaf-litter below. These species are a sign that this is a relic of a very ancient forest, since they do not spread easily, and tend to occur only in woodlands which have had a long, undisturbed history.

Another frequent relic is the ancient hedgerow. As the town grew, land would be developed field by field, ownership after ownership. The old hedgerows inevitably became the front line, dividing one stage of development from the next. Often they were left intact, to form the back garden boundary between housing estates, or the edge of a new school playing field. Although the thorn and field maple have now grown leggy with neglect, and have often been replaced altogether by neat and tidy Larchlap fencing, the hedgerow trees remain – too expensive to remove from amongst the buildings, and an important string of stepping stones for birds and insects as they move around the town.

Heathland is another surprisingly common relic habitat in towns. The names of Birmingham's suburbs – Kings Heath,

Small Heath, Bourneheath – are a clear reminder of the landscape that preceded Brum. Sure enough, if you look closely, particularly on land isolated by the early railways, you can find spectacular examples of heathland habitat, with banks of ling and heather, bushes of bilberry, and a thin sprinkling of silver birch. Where the heathland relic is big enough, island colonies of heathland insects have survived too, though the merlin, the golden plover and the sand lizard have not been spotted there for many a year. They need much bigger territories than the town can offer.

There are some wonderful relic wetlands in our towns too. Lakes and marshes do tend to silt up quite rapidly, and so much of the land which was too wet to build on in the early nineteenth century has since been gobbled up on return visits, but much wetland does survive, and this is often deeply hidden behind the factories and houses. In Knutsford, there is wetland on a grand scale, with the mock-Mediterranean houses of this little Cheshire town looking out over the broad reedbeds and duck-covered waters of the Mere. In Chester, the riverside meadows, which flood every winter, have survived as a wild, green wetland plugging deep into the heart of the city, whilst in nearby Wigan, Orwell's fictional pier was sited in a landscape which is still a mysterious wet wilderness of canals, swamps and reedbeds. On a much smaller scale, Moseley Bog in Birmingham is typical of thousands of pockets of swampy land, often covered with willow and alder, and still providing a nesting site for summer visitors such as the willow warbler and the chiffchaff, as it must have done for centuries before the city surrounded it.

Moseley Bog is particularly interesting, because it was actually recognised as an important wetland wildlife site a century or more ago. There are reams of records of rare sedges, ferns and other wet woodland species, collected by Victorian boffins and lovingly described. For years, no-one connected these old records of 'the natural history of Moseley Bog' with the patch of magical wet woodland that everyone knew as 'the dingle', 'the dell', or just 'that nice place behind the houses'. When the site was inevitably threatened with development, the locals did a bit more digging, put two and two together, and came to the conclusion that this was indeed the once famous Moseley Bog. Thanks to their enthusiasm and energy, the bog was spared, and so the summer songbirds and rare plants like the giant horsetail and royal fern can continue to enjoy their watery urban oasis.

Plants with fluffy, wind-blown seed are quick to colonise urban wasteland. This thistle may not be everyone's idea of a glamorous wildflower, but its flowers are full of nectar – good for insects – and small birds enjoy the seeds in early autumn.

These very old relic sites are important because they often contain rare species which can't cope with change. Bluebells and harebells simply can't dodge around from site to site, and so each time an ancient woodland or a heathland is damaged, much of its resident wildlife disappears forever. By contrast, there are many other sites in towns whose main virtue is the way in which they are constantly disturbed and stirred up. Demolition and redevelopment have always been a feature of our towns. Many of those plants and animals that thrived in the old, unsprayed arable farmland for so many centuries have now taken up residence on disturbed urban wasteland. In fact, with such intensity of cropping and the spectacular increase in farm weedkillers, the city is the safest place to be if you are a poppy or a thistle. The main characteristic of these wasteland plant communities is their ability to achieve rapid pollination, and then to distribute their offspring. Flowers tend to be bright, and seeds are produced in huge numbers. As a result there are clouds of attendant insects in the summer, and then flocks of seed-eating finches through the autumn and winter. Goldfinches in particular are a feature of these urban weed patches, and I've seen charms of over fifty of these happy sounding little birds glittering their way through the thistles on sites in deepest Brixton. Another less glamorous feature of these short-life wastelands is the

Charms of goldfinches will move around the town, feeding on the seed of wasteland plants such as this teasel.

rubbish that gets dumped there. Although fly-tipping looks awful, and tends to give such places a bad image, a great many aggressive garden throw-outs end up there as a result, and such plants as golden rod, Michaelmas daisy and raspberry add enormously to the colourfulness of the habitat, and to the food available for local wildlife.

Some of those used and abused disturbance sites never do get redeveloped. Perhaps the most important wildlife resource of all, particularly in our older industrial cities, is the land which was exploited by past industries and left for dead perhaps fifty or a hundred years ago. Both the quantity and the quality of this so-called derelict land is spectacular. Many of the sites must have resembled glacial moraine when they were first abandoned, but with time they go through all the stages I described in chapter two, beginning with the wind-borne pioneers, and as the soils develop, they evolve a woodland canopy. The explosive growth and resulting inefficiency of the industrial use often meant that there were tiny pockets of land amongst the pit heaps, the demolition rubble and the industrial waste which managed to survive quite undisturbed by 'progress'. In many cases, seventy or a hundred years of total neglect have allowed these fragments to recolonise their neighbouring dereliction, and the wildflowers and insects can sometimes be startlingly rich. Very often the nature of the dereliction actually helps make the wildlife special. I can think of several sites, for instance, where gravel and sand have been quarried, or where shallow coal-mining has taken place. In all these cases, what the industrialists left behind was a lumpy site with no soil, and just a layer of grit and stone for plants to colonise. As a result, the only plants that could really cope were members of the pea-family. Various vetches and clovers now form a continuous sheet over the surface of the ground, able to survive despite its poverty, through their ability to trap their own fertiliser from the air in the form of nitrogen. These sites are extremely pretty through the summer, with white clover, purple vetch and yellow birdsfoot trefoil all intermingled. There is usually a thriving population of common blue butterflies to add to the kaleidoscope, laying their eggs on the trefoil leaves and sipping the nectar from the flowers.

Where the rubble is coarser, but soil is still absent, the pioneers are often silver birch and goat willow. Both these woody colonisers are able to produce millions of light, wind-borne seed from their fourth or fifth year onwards. So

just one surviving specimen upwind of a freshly disturbed or
demolished site is enough to provide sufficient seed for a
whole new pioneer woodland. Both these species are
particularly good food plants for a wide range of caterpillars and
other plant-eating creepy-crawlies such as shield-bugs, so
they inevitably attract large flocks of small birds – particularly
in spring when there are hatchlings to be fed.

If the derelict site has soil of any description on it, then it
seems inevitably to develop a cover of bramble and thorn
scrub. It is pretty difficult to find a good blackberry patch in
the farming countryside these days, but there are hundreds
of acres of what amounts to hawthorn and wild rose woodland
throughout our industrial cities. These types of landscape
are particularly rich in wildlife. The pockets of unsprayed
grassland support large populations of small mammals, and
so attract predators such as the tawny owl, the weasel and the
inevitable kestrel. The thorn scrub produces a spectacular
display of may blossom in the spring, and a huge harvest of
haws in autumn. The spiny nature of so many of these
grassland pioneers makes them relatively safe sites for songbird
nest-building, too. Perhaps the most breathtaking wildlife
spectacle of all on urban wasteland sites is to see a flock of
two or three thousand redwings and fieldfares, freshly
arrived from Northern Scandinavia, gorging themselves on a
crimson crop of hawthorn berries. I watched just such a
sight one January, right in the middle of the Black Country,
and on that occasion had the extra thrill of seeing all three
thousand birds take off simultaneously, as a sparrowhawk
streaked amongst them, and wiped out the one which was
just a bit too slow.

There really is so much of this old industrial wild space, it
is not surprising that it has been rather taken for granted.
It teems not only with wildlife, but with kids as well, off on
their tracking bikes with a fishing net and jam jar or perhaps
a 'borrowed' box of matches. There is often an element of
danger in these landscapes too, and that adds spice to the
adventures enjoyed there. These unofficial users add greatly
to the richness of the habitat. Our young adventurer with
the matches is quite likely to go just a bit too far, and burn
off a patch of dead grass or an overgrown gorse bush. Next
spring, up through the charcoal-blackened scar will spring
willowherb, fresh gorse shoots, and perhaps a grateful sprig
or two of almost-suffocated heather.

The scramble-bikers who cause so much annoyance to the

Urban kestrels have soared in numbers since the war. The combination of tall buildings for nest-sites and wild, unsprayed grassland for hunting suits this predator perfectly.

quieter neighbours, whilst thoughtlessly churning up the wet hollows, may well be providing nest-building mud for house martins and songthrushes. The constant buzz of their bikes could even be seen as benefiting wildlife, by driving other users away and so actually reducing the kind of disturbance that really bothers nesting birds such as the linnet and the dunnock. I knew one particularly noisy site in the south of England, where both nightingales and wrens seemed to thrive on the competition, and sang louder than usual.

The piles of lawn clippings and other festering unmentionables that come oozing out of enormous black plastic bags boost fertility in the soil and foster great sheets of stinging nettles. These may help keep prying feet from disturbance beyond, and they provide a vital source of larval food for the caterpillars of some of our most colourful garden butterflies.

Over the last twenty years or so, particularly since the Aberfan disaster when a coal waste tip slipped in a rain storm, and buried a school full of little children, thousands of acres of this rich urban wilderness have been swept away in 'environmental improvement schemes'. The 'hills and mountains', the wet bits and the stony bits, the brambles and hawthorn have all been flattened and transformed into yet more bright green, safe, respectable sterile deserts. This 'landscaping', so called, has deprived a great many townspeople of their only real contact with wild nature, and in many local authorities the practice still continues. In recent years, a much more sensitive approach has been developed, pioneered by specialist groups of engineers and landscape architects in such blighted areas as the West Midlands, South Yorkshire and Wigan. Regrettably, much of this expertise has been thrown away with the abolition of the Metropolitan County Councils, but with luck, we will manage to cling on to some of the accumulated skills, and at least part of this huge wild resource will continue to be reclaimed with sensitivity. The very best examples of reclamation are those where the landscape has been taken seriously, managed with care, but still allowed to develop naturally. With just one or two perceptive, skilled professionals coaxing the landscape along, and at the same time fostering care in the community, the difference is remarkable. Rubbish dumping dwindles, birds' nests are left unrobbed, mums and dads feel safer letting children play, and the wildlife thrives. There are confusing problems to be tackled, though. Even with the most skilful supervision, how do you maintain the programme of haphazard, accidental burning that did so much in the past to promote habitat diversity? These landscapes have resulted from a whole string of happy accidents. It is very difficult indeed to make sure that these accidents continue to happen.

One particularly interesting example of the forces that shape these landscapes can be found on urban wasteland close to where I live.

There are several huge patches of lumpy, undulating wilderness, created by shallow mining, subsidence and uncontrolled tipping. Over the past century an interesting and complex mosaic of hawthorn and bramble islands and cropped grass clearings has developed. The reason for such a striking vegetation pattern is quite complex. The scrap metal merchants of the Black Country have always tethered

You have more chance of seeing poppies in the town than in the countryside. These colourful 'weeds' thrive on disturbance, but are easily killed by agricultural chemicals. No-one is spraying the demolition rubble with weedkiller.

their ponies here overnight. The ponies were staked out in a grassy glade, with their wandering restricted by a length of rope or chain. The circles they grazed remained free from thorns. The bits they couldn't reach developed as scrub. That process of casual management has gone on throughout most of this century, but now, suddenly, everything has changed, and the diversity of wildlife habitat is suffering. Most of those unofficial grazers, the scrap men, had a ready market for their iron and steel in Round Oak Steelworks, just up the road. This was one of the few foundries that relied heavily on scrap iron as a basic raw material. In 1981 Round Oak was closed. Thousands of locals were made redundant, and one of the knock-on casualties was the scrap business. In no time at all many of the ponies were trotting off towards the dining tables of Belgium, the grazing stopped, and within a couple of years the thorn was leaping into the grassy glades, and taking over. That change is good for the redwings and fieldfares, but not so good for the grasshoppers, the grass snakes, the bank voles and the kestrels. If the habitat mosaic is to be conserved, then the managers have to find a viable alternative to casual grazing by totters' ponies. Maybe a riding centre for local children, or a community-based city farm could provide the answer.

There is another green land-use in towns which makes almost as great a contribution to wildlife as the derelict wildscape. Large settlements of people tend to create a need for all kinds of services and some of them produce interesting landscapes and rather special habitats. I'm thinking of such extensive land uses as refuse tips, sewage works, reservoirs and airports.

The waste we generate provides rich pickings for a whole range of wild animals. Our sewage filter beds are attended by hordes of insect-eating birds through the summer months. Tens of thousands of house martins, swifts and swallows leave the sunshine of Africa every spring, to spend their summer hols snapping up midges over our city sewage works, and where the effluent is allowed to flow into settlement lagoons, flocks of waders gather every winter to feed knee deep in smelly sludge. There's no accounting for taste.

The raucous sound of squabbling gulls, screaming over juicy bits of refuse, is a noisy reminder of the important role scavengers play in the natural world. These gulls have turned their back on the sea, and now, instead of wheeling in clouds behind the fishing boats to catch the guts and offal thrown overboard, they have moved to the other end of the system, and sort through the salmon tins and chip wrappers of the rubbish tips for their tasty morsels instead.

When these gulls are off duty, many of them spend their time bobbing up and down in the middle of our reservoirs, out of harm's way. These man-made lakes have become important over the years, not so much as breeding sites for wildlife, but as winter rest-stops for a whole host of ducks, geese and swans. There is many an eager birdwatcher who has spotted that first real rarity whilst surrounded by a battery of binoculars, telephoto lenses and telescopes on the edge of Frankley, Brent or Chew reservoir.

The pattern of daily gull migration has, in fact, created a serious problem, particularly in London. As luck would have it, Heathrow sits in between a group of reservoirs and a group of waste dumps. Every day, squawking flocks of gulls commute backwards and forwards across the flight path, playing Russian roulette with the jet engines. Not surprisingly, the GLC's ecologists are suddenly being taken rather more seriously now it can be seen that their advice may perhaps save lives, and the siting of waste dumps and reservoirs is being planned with gull commuter patterns in mind.

The last great land resource which needs a very special mention is the million or so acres of private gardens in Britain. They may not be so significant deep in the core of the commercial centre of town, but gardens do create an immense outer ring of woodland glade habitat, separating that core from the green belt and the countryside. Gardens are important, too, because they represent a huge amount of land which ordinary individuals like you and me can actually manage for ourselves. Together, the gardens of a neighbourhood can provide a happy hunting ground for wanderers like the hedgehog and the weasel, but even an individual garden, if it is managed without chemicals, allowed to grow a little untidy, and filled with the right plants, can provide a permanent home for a surprising range of wild plants and animals.

There is no doubt about it. The green spaces of our towns and cities are the most important wildlife reserve this country has got. I hope I've convinced you that the scale of the landscape resource is enormous. The richness of the wildlife itself constantly amazes me, but most important of all, these particular wild places are right on your doorstep – so the obvious thing to do is to get out there and start looking.

This must beat Force 8 gales in the North Sea. The nearest these 'seagulls' get to the ocean is a sardine-tin on the local refuse tip.

LUXURY LIFESTYLE
FOR CITY WILDLIFE

4

The green space in towns and cities is much more than a simple, slightly degraded duplicate of pre-war farmland. For a great many species, the town is a much better place to live in than the countryside ever was.

It's warmer for a start. The heat leaking out from all those poorly-insulated buildings combines with that from the engines of thousands of traffic-jammed cars, lorries and buses, and the warm bodies of the crowds of people. Much of that warm air is trapped amongst the buildings, and this generally means that it is at least one or two degrees warmer than it would be at the same time in the surrounding countryside. This heat bonus has two effects on the wildlife. Firstly, on very cold nights it can mean that fewer individuals freeze to death, and during long, cold spells the insect-eaters and the water-based wildlife have shorter periods without food. Secondly, it means that southern species, particularly plants, can extend their range just that little bit further north. A wildflower or insect which is just on the northern edge of its range in rural Oxfordshire, for example, may well be able to survive a hundred miles further north in the relative urban warmth of Sheffield or Manchester.

The most dramatic demonstration of this heat-pool effect of towns can be seen in every big city at the end of each winter's day. We have about thirty-five million starlings in Britain. Five million of those are resident all year round,

Millions of Soviet starlings fly to Britain each year, to enjoy our warmer winter. They feed in the countryside by day, and migrate to centrally-heated city roosts each evening. How can people fail to see how spectacularly beautiful their nightly performance is?

but the other thirty million spend the summer breeding in the farmland of eastern bloc countries such as Poland and the USSR. Those countries even have a major nest-box programme, aimed at increasing the starling population, since they value them so much as a safe, non-toxic pesticide squad. Why on earth do we in the west turn our back on such obvious good sense?

Starlings visit Britain from October to March, to enjoy our warmer winter climate, and every evening millions of them commute from feeding grounds in our countryside and the mown grasslands of our parks and playing fields, to spend the night huddled together on the window ledges and neon signs of their centrally heated roosts in the city. Their arrival each evening must be one of the most spectacular sights of the natural world. Tens of thousands of these birds will sweep and curve their way through the air, moving in strict unison, and looking for all the world like a wisp of black smoke, or one of those cartoon swarms of bees that plague the life out of Tom, Yogi and Co. The daily performance usually lasts fifteen to twenty minutes, and rises to a crescendo as the birds swoop nearer and nearer, and drop excitedly on to their chosen ledges. Suddenly the invisible thread which held the squadron together is snipped. The tight pattern collapses and each bird is an individual again, chattering noisily to anyone who will listen, about the latest line in leatherjackets, and where the pickings were richest that day.

Anyone who visited Leicester Square, London, in the winter of 1985/86 would have had a dramatic reminder that not everyone shares my total enthusiasm for commuter starlings. It is true, of course, that they do make quite a racket for an hour or so before they settle down for the night, and it is also true that they make rather a mess of the pavement – especially at the beginning of autumn when elderberries feature high on the menu and paving stones turn purple.

Inevitably, so much 'nature' in one living mass is too much for a certain kind of town-dweller, and so all sorts of tactics have been adopted to try and drive the starlings away. Some councils have applied the big bang theory. Others have taken professional advice, and played recordings of the starlings' alarm call. Many buildings, including the Houses of Parliament, have been criss-crossed with wire, to keep the birds off ledges, and some ledges have been daubed with a sticky paste which no self-respecting starling would want to stand in for long. In Leicester Square, so angry was the

anti-starling lobby, that all these weapons were combined, and
the screeches and bangs were accompanied by the beating
of dustbin lids, blowing of whistles and a great deal of ritual
arm waving. Needless to say, the starlings looked on in quiet
amusement. They co-operated from time to time, of course,
by fluttering half-heartedly from one side of the square to
the other, whilst dismissing any hope of all-out victory the
protestors might have had with a well-aimed dollop or two
of their own 'secret weapon'. The noise and inconvenience
caused by 'the beaters' was considerably more offensive than
anything the birds produced. Inevitably, in true British
tradition, a pro-starling lobby quickly emerged, pressing
cyclostyled S.O.S. ('Save Our Starlings') leaflets into the
hands of bemused Japanese tourists and late-for-the-show
theatregoers.

Eventually, the noisy protestors admitted defeat. This secret
army from beyond the Iron Curtain had achieved another
moral victory and peace returned to Leicester Square – peace,
that is, except for the constant roar of the traffic, and the
slightly smug Siberian chatter of the starlings.

If you think of big buildings as cliffs, which is undoubtedly
the way that birds see them, then it is not surprising to find
quite a range of species have adopted them. Kestrels, for
instance, have been breeding on the top of tower blocks
since the late 1950s, and no doubt they nested on church
steeples for centuries before that. More recently, the
peregrine falcon, another cliff-nesting bird of prey, has
become a tower-block dweller with a nesting site in
Manchester that has been used for several seasons. The
peregrine was close to extinction not so long ago, following the
combined pressure of agro-chemicals, and a war-time
programme of near genocide. Peregrines chase, catch, kill
and eat pigeons. During the war they were a serious threat to
military intelligence, as carrier pigeons with vital messages
from behind enemy lines were wiped out by falcons over the
White Cliffs of Dover. Now, of course, these superb birds
are the subject of a major military operation of a different
kind, as the RSPB mounts its annual nest-watch to try and
protect today's peregrines from egg-robbers. If these
spectacular hunters do move into our towns, and begin to
breed successfully on our town halls and railway stations, then
certainly they will have no difficulty in finding the odd
pigeon or two to feed on. They take starlings on the wing too,
so maybe that is the answer to the Leicester Square problem.

There was a time when the rock-dove nested exclusively on cliffs – but as it became urbanised, the town pigeon recognised the buildings of the High Street as housing accommodation, with a ready supply of tame humans to provide bed and breakfast.

The heat from buildings is used by a great many other wild creatures apart from starlings. Town pigeons often share the window ledges, and they will build their nests there too, given half a chance. There are a great many accounts of urban foxes which have gone one stage further, and curl up right outside the outlet vent from the heating system, to be wafted with a draught of warmed air, day or night. Opportunist species like these have always done well living alongside man.

The wildlife that lives in or around water can be particularly badly affected by cold weather. Most water plans avoid the problem by dying away in the autumn, and lurking as a rootstock or a seed, safe in the mud until spring. Many of the animals adopt much the same tactic, with frogs overwintering sound asleep, buried in the bottom of their pond, and newts creeping away from the water in late summer and hibernating under a log or deep in the crevice of a brick wall until the warmer weather returns. Birds don't hibernate, indeed they have to keep eating without fail right through the winter. If the water is frozen over for much more than a day, then birds such as the heron and the moorhen will move away from the ice, and feed wherever they can find soft ground. Herons will switch from fish to other food such as earthworms, and even carrion in order to survive. Some species are not so lucky, though. If they are totally dependent on water-based food, then they either move elsewhere or they die. The kingfisher is a colourful case in point. As the streams and ponds of the countryside begin to freeze over, these beautiful little birds migrate in large numbers to the coast. Here, the warming influence of the sea and the brackish saltiness of much of the water mean that there is more chance of finding an ice-free hunting site, even if the food does come ready-salted. At the end of the winter, the survivors move back inland to breed. Nevertheless, a great many kingfishers die every winter, and the population has been reduced by as much as a third in really bad years. The inner city offers a very convenient alternative to a winter by the windswept seashore. The canals and park lakes, the rivers and streams are all warmed by that same heat-pool that encourages the roosting starlings, and quite often there is heat pumped directly into the water, as sewage outflows and industrial cooling water outlets pour warmed water into an adjacent river or canal. This extra warmth is good for the fish population, and certainly there is no shortage of shoals of minnows in the inner city canals, for instance, but most importantly for the kingfisher, there are always gaps to be found in the ice, and no end of bridges, pipes and cables from which to dive into the food-rich water. There are urban populations of kingfishers in many of our cities now, and their increase is restricted not by cold water or lack of food, but by a shortage of suitable secluded cliff-hole nesting-sites.

All this leaking warmth can be a disadvantage to species such as the small mammals that hibernate to survive the winter. Some of them really do need to be cold to stay dormant and conserve their fat reserves. Pipistrelle bats, for example, choose a hot spot for summer breeding, but when autumn comes, and their insect food simply runs out, they move to cold, north-facing winter quarters, their metabolism slows right down, and they effectively switch off until the spring. It's easy to see how the empty building they choose in autumn might suddenly warm up if new human tenants move in and turn on the heating in midwinter. The bats would wake up to a false spring, with no hope of food and little chance of survival. Artificial bat-boxes on the outside of buildings don't run the risk of a midwinter warm-up, so we should be providing many more of them.

These long-eared bats are perfectly happy roosting in a building rather than a cave or hollow tree. They are protected by law, but still seriously threatened by poisoning if the wrong treatment is applied to the beams.

Simple batboxes really work. Choose a cold, north-facing site for winter hibernation and a hot, south-facing position for summer nursery roosts.

Plants, too, can be lured into a premature flowering, or early leaf, and then get clobbered by a very severe cold wind with a biting chill factor. Generally speaking, though, the warmth of a city benefits its wildlife.

I talked in chapter one about my childhood landscape, with its wildscape and close contact with nature. I didn't mention the many evenings when I would walk home from cubs in a fog so thick that I really couldn't see from one lamp-post to the next. I lived in Sheffield, and the smoke and grime of the steel industry was particularly bad, but industrial pollution was a feature of most towns and cities, and the uncontrolled burning of coal in millions of domestic fireplaces had a dramatic and damaging effect on the environment. As well as the obvious blackening of buildings, the 'peasoupers', the constant sound of bronchitic coughing, and the need for 'no spitting' signs on buses, the quality and quantity of wildlife also suffered seriously. Some insects, most notably the peppered moth, exhibited industrial melanism, evolving from a light to a dark colour, gradually, over several generations, and so blending more successfully with their soot-blackened surroundings. Most species simply didn't survive at all, and as insect populations declined, swifts and swallows, wrens and flycatchers failed to find food, and so the music hall image of the coughing sparrow was established as the sole representative of nature in the city.

Things are very different now. In thirty years the whole situation has been dramatically reversed. Now one of the great attractions of city living is the lack of chemical pollution. The Clean Air Act eliminated smoke and fog as effectively as a giant extractor fan. Other pollution controls slowly cleaned up our urban waterways, and people began to breathe fresh air again. During that same thirty year period, whilst society was cleaning up its act in the towns, chemical pollution was devastating wildlife in the countryside. The new agricultural revolution was founded on a seemingly limitless supply of inorganic fertiliser, pesticides, herbicides and fungicides, all applied with gay abandon at first, by post-war farmers who were told by the government to 'increase production at all costs'. Newly-invented chemicals were fed into the environment. These began innocently enough by killing harmful pests, but they quickly fed their way up the food chain, affecting one harmless species after another, until eventually, predators such as the golden eagle and the sparrowhawk were driven to extinction in large areas of their original territory.

The worst period, particularly for the organochlorines, was in the 1960s. These were the persistent pesticides such as aldrin, dieldrin and DDT which were added to the soil or sprayed on to crops to control pests. The problem was that they were designed never to go away. When the research scientists first began to realise that there was a serious knock-on effect in the wider countryside, programmes were set up to monitor the damage. Quite often whole families of badger corpses would be brought to the laboratory – mum, dad and two or three cubs. Time and again when the dead animals were opened up, their stomachs were found to be full of newly-eaten wood-pigeons, laced with a heavy dose of pesticide. The explanation was simple. Farmers treated their seed-corn with organochlorines, and pigeons pecked away on the farm, picking up an overdose of poison. The poison was stored in their fatty tissues during the daytime, and then at night, when the birds were roosting in the woods, these contaminated fat reserves were used up, the chemical entered the bloodstream and one by one the birds would drop from the trees. Badgers will eat most things, and whilst they normally feed mainly on earthworms, they couldn't possibly resist such a tasty feast as a fresh pigeon. Bird after bird would be snapped up by the foraging badger family, and by the following morning the badgers too would be dead: another case of mass murder for the scientists to unravel.

The farming scene is a bit better now. Farmers have learned to be more accurate, there are stricter controls on methods of application, and the worst of the chemicals have been banned in Britain, though many of them are still sold abroad, to continue their devastation amongst the innocents of the developing world. Some of the worst chemicals are still available to domestic gardeners in this country, too, and certainly aldrin, one of the most damaging of the persistent pesticides, is used extensively in the soil you buy your pot-grown shrubs in from the garden centre. All the harmful chemicals that were used in those early days are still there in our environment too, of course. The whole point about them is that they simply don't go away. They will continue to travel around the food webs forever.

The pesticide poisons are not the only agricultural chemicals to damage wildlife. Nitrogen fertiliser run-off is so contaminating some of the streams and rivers of East Anglia that there is very serious concern about their continuing suitability for drinking water supply. Daily deliveries of bottled drinking water along with the milk may not be so far away.

So whether we like it or not, our intensive farming countryside is now more polluted with chemicals than much of the green space in our cities. Only rarely is anyone spraying the railway embankments with pesticides. No one is emptying sacks of nitrogenous fertiliser into the canals, and not surprisingly, as towns have been cleaned up, wildlife has benefited. The reason our Victorian parks were planted exclusively with laurel bushes and carpet bedding was simple. A hundred years ago – even fifty years ago – they were the only plants that could survive the air pollution. Now the urban flora is probably richer than ever before. We have butterflies in our urban grasslands, swifts and swallows overhead, dragonflies breeding in our urban wetlands, and if we could just stop stupidly applying agricultural chemicals to the green deserts of our road verges, parks and playing fields, we would have near perfection. Pesticide-free zones might be a much more useful political initiative than nuclear-free zones, and certainly they are more realistically achievable. In West Germany, Switzerland and Sweden that is exactly what has happened in dozens of towns and cities. Weedkillers are banned. There may be a few more tufts of grass around the base of the lamp-posts. There are probably many more dandelions in the road verges. That may irritate the more tidy-minded citizens, but even they have decided that a little untidiness is preferable to the hidden dangers of a landscape sprayed with poison.

Where wildlife is concerned, chemical pollution is far and away the biggest threat to most species, and from that point of view life in the city is pretty good.

One thing I find particularly fascinating about wildlife in towns, is the way that the landscape is so tightly interwoven with people's lives. Every corner of every settlement is full of fascinating ghosts, and the wildlife is so often a direct link to the past. If you sit in the 'new' Covent Garden, throwing crumbs of your all-American blueberry cheesecake or your sticky so-called Danish pastry to the sparrows, take a long, hard look at your feathered companions. They are the great-great-great-great . . . grandsons and daughters of sparrows that stole from the nosebags of the ranks of draught horses, which stood patiently waiting to make the long haul back to the cabbage fields of the nineteenth century countryside. Some of their more recent ancestors would have

fed on the sandwiches dropped by the demolition workers who brought the fruit and vegetable era to an end, and way back in time, earlier members of that same long line of sparrows would probably have been there to pick up scraps from the kitchens of the Romans who first began to shape London.

Much nearer home, how many of my house's previous occupants have thrilled, as I do, to the scream of the swifts returning from a warm winter in Africa, to nest under the eaves? That same family of swifts, generation after generation, has been flying backwards and forwards between the Dark Continent and this very house, for over seventy years, and so they have sustained an intimate relationship with generations of different human residents. There are examples in London and elsewhere, of ancient badger setts which have been entirely encircled by housing, and where after countless generations of country living, Brock and Co. have adapted successfully to their bourgeois new life among the privet hedges, garden lawns and dustbins of suburbia.

That hedgehog which you consider to be your own personal wild creature, has an uninterrupted ancestry which stretches back on your patch of the earth, for over 7000 years, to the wooded landscape of Stone Age man the hunter-gatherer.

Old cemeteries and churchyards have become very important sanctuaries for city wildlife – and they are full of clues to the local history too. If there is a wild burial ground in your neighbourhood, adopt it quickly, before it is 'tidied' out of existence.

Some urban landscapes very obviously bring nature and history together. Cemeteries, for example, are frequently an important wildlife resource, their hallowed ground being protected from any threat of building. Some of the wildest are those which were created in the middle of the last century, to serve the industrial middle classes. They have a great array of ornate monuments, stone angels and a magnificent mausoleum or two, and these provide a wealth of nooks and crannies for more secretive wildlife. Many of these private cemeteries had a very short life, if you see what I mean, and were often opened for business and then sold out within the space of a decade. By the turn of this century most of their ornate gates had been locked shut and nature took over behind the high walls and iron railings. Over the past sixty or seventy years they have become more and more tangled and overgrown, and now it is often quite difficult to find the stately avenues and sad inscriptions under the jungle of bramble, sycamore and ivy.

There is an interesting new threat to these particular urban wild spaces now. They are all too often becoming the subject of clean-up campaigns. Temporary employment scheme leaders seem to like nothing better than to move in a team of fit youngsters, to rip out the undergrowth, lift and transfer the headstones and monuments to the edge of the site, and put the hallowed ground down to neat, tidy, boring mown turf. It's happening everywhere, with no regard either for the wildlife these places support, or for the history tied up in the headstones. I saw a terrible example of this in Hull recently where in the space of three months a group of eager but misdirected youngsters had laid waste a fascinating patch of wild history, and produced in its place yet another characterless mowing-machine landscape. Such official vandalism can be stopped if you try hard enough. Beckett Street Cemetery in Leeds is just such a wild place. This was threatened with the same sort of sterile respectability, but the 'Friends of Beckett Street Cemetery' were determined that the place should survive, and after a struggle, it has remained wild. It now enjoys just a little more care and attention, and a good deal of creative use by local schools. In this case, as with so many others, it was the social value of the landscape, as much as its resident wildlife, which won the day. An amateur historian took the trouble to show how you can trace the fortunes of various local families simply by reading the headstones in the cemetery. A proud sense of history prevailed and the wildlife benefited as a result. If the 'improvers' hadn't been stopped, then the foxes, owls, bats, wrens, comma butterflies, violets, brambles and other wild plants and animals would have been made homeless – and Leeds would have lost another bit of its commonplace history.

Not all the links with local history are as obvious as those in a cemetery, but nevertheless they are there if you look. In many parts of industrial Britain there are barren patches of land where nothing grows at all. These are often all that remains of an evil-smelling chemical works that formed the basis for an entire local economy. In the coalfields there are numerous pockets of 'lumpy' land, uncultivated and uncared for. These may be the sites of the very earliest mining operations, where the bell-pits were sunk down into the coal seam, and then worked sideways with pick and shovel to the point when the bell-shaped hole became unstable. All this undermining left this land too dangerous for anyone to interfere with it again, and so the wildlife moved in and thrived. I know a marvellous meadow with just this kind of background, near Barnsley. It is too lumpy and unsafe to cultivate, and as a result it has developed a fabulous community of meadow flowers. Field scabious, mallow, knapweed and bedstraw grow in the deeper pockets of soil, and colourful sheets of birdsfoot trefoil, harebell and meadow bindweed cover the thin gravelly soils of the excavation mounds. This is the best site I know for unusual moths and there are always owls, kestrels, bats and swallows hunting there in the summer.

On a grander scale, there are large sheets of shallow water in many mining areas, known as 'flashes'. These wetlands tend to come and go over the years, and they too are usually the result of mining subsidence. As whole sections of deep workings collapse, the land above settles, or, as the engineers so practically put it, 'the voids migrate to the surface'. If there is water in the area, the hollow floods and another flash is formed. Some of these wetlands are enormously important to wildlife, even though they may be very new. Nature reserves such as Fairburn Ings in South Yorkshire and Alvecote pools on the Staffordshire/Warwickshire border were created this way. In parts of Cheshire and north Worcestershire there are settlement flashes, caused not by coal-mining, but by salt extraction.

Here the salinity of the resulting wetland habitats enables plants to grow which are otherwise almost exclusively coastal.

These include such species as sea aster, sea milkwort, and sea spurrey, and the sites are very important indeed in natural history terms.

Mining collapse is quite a subtle way of forming a hole in the surface of the earth. There are, of course, plenty of examples of more directly man-made holes. Quarries, clay pits and gravel pits are a dramatic feature of many of our urban areas. Some, like the gravel pits at Rickmansworth for example, are extremely ancient, and probably Roman in origin. Many are still being created as the demand for concrete and road building grinds relentlessly on. Quarries are of limited value whilst still being dug, but once disturbance ceases, then nature moves in and re-enacts the post-glacial stages of colonisation. Birch and willow are there in no time, and within as little as five or six years a dry sand quarry or a clay pit can have turned into dense scrub.

These new, barren landscapes can often throw up extremely rare plants – simply because in the wild such open, thinly vegetated sites are very uncommon indeed. There may be rare species of fungi, for instance, and some of the purple orchids in particular are frequently to be found growing in abundance. The public image of 'orchids' is that they are very rare, and only grow in ancient, undisturbed places. That is certainly true of some species – the monkey, man and spider orchids for instance, but purple and spotted orchids love freshly disturbed wet clays, and that most spectacular of plants, the bee orchid, is a pioneer of well-drained sandy soils. The seed of these beautiful wildflowers is as fine as dust, and so they are quite capable of blowing around and landing on freshly cleared sites.

When they do, the lack of competition means they often flourish. The artificial sand mountains of St Helens, on Merseyside, thrown up as a by-product of the glass industry, are covered in sheets of purple orchids. In Northamptonshire's clay pits and sand quarries I have seen acre upon acre of bright yellow birdsfoot trefoil, and dozens of bee orchids, too. In Kent, there are numerous chalk quarries, excavated to make cement. The oldest of these have developed an interesting, very thin chalky soil on the quarry floor, and with the help of grazing wild rabbits, there is a downland flora developing, close-cropped and crammed with dozens of different species of wildflowers. With a little assistance, many of these poor, infertile, industrial 'holes' could become wonderful sanctuaries for wildflowers and the

This little patch of ground is in the heart of a huge housing estate in London. When I cultivated it, for the first time since the war, crowds of cornfield weeds burst into life. The seeds they grew from had fallen in the days when this patch of London was still green fields – instant history.

Early purple orchids by the thousand. Pilkington's Glass Works have built mountains of waste sand in the middle of St Helens, and unintentionally provided the ideal habitat for these beautiful wild flowers.

butterflies and other insects they support. Until recently, they have been seen exclusively as eyesores, but with considerable commercial value as land-fill sites. Now some of them are actually being designated as official nature reserves instead.

Wet gravel pits appeared in the flood plains of many of our lowland rivers, to help feed the boom in post-war motorways and concrete buildings. By digging down below the water-table, such excavations automatically become lakes, and in time these can develop extremely rich wildlife populations. The quarrying company Amey Roadstone Ltd realised very early on that this 'dereliction' had positive potential for wildlife and water-sports, and that with a little help their massive machinery could carry out refinements to their pits which would help speed up revegetation. They

Granite setts by a Leeds canal. Mosses and weed-seedlings make a pretty pattern in the cracks – but the real magic lies with the 'ghosts' who clatter across the cobbles – and the beautiful detail that is everywhere in towns if you care to look.

have funded a research unit, managed by the Game Conservancy, on the shores of a gravel pit at Great Linford in Milton Keynes, and it is their industrially funded research which is the basis of some of the techniques I will discuss in chapter nine.

The particular way in which town-dwelling man has used a patch of land can often have a direct effect on the wildlife there. I don't just mean disturbance leading to pioneer vegetation. There are more direct links than that. If you look around our city waste-tips, for instance, you can find a whole range of strange plants growing. Some will have arrived as seed with the sand-trays from the cages of the 'Pretty Joey' budgies. Others will have grown from the vegetable peelings of an Anglo-oriental kitchen. Whatever their origin, they will still be there growing in the landscape, when the tip is covered over, grassed down and long forgotten. I wonder what the wide-eyed botanists of the future might make of the sweet potato, millet and cannabis plants that turn up in their surveys.

In a similar way, you can see unusual plants growing in the walls around our older docks. Look for a slightly crumbly south-facing stone wall in St Katharine's Dock, or Southampton Dock, Hull or Liverpool, and you will find tropical weeds growing – descendants, perhaps, of early settlers brought as seed amongst the deck cargo of the tea clippers or the slave ships.

The older landscapes are just full of these little clues to the past. An old apple tree and a tangle of rambling roses beside the canal will mark the spot where a lock-keeper's cottage once stood. A sheet of silver birch all exactly the same age will mark out precisely the shape of the railway shunting yard which was stripped to its ash and hardcore thirty years ago and colonised immediately by clouds of wind-borne birch seed. Lime-loving wildflowers like the cranesbill and the kidney-vetch will suddenly crop up in the midst of an otherwise acidic landscape – evidence of an old limestone-crushing plant for the steelworks, or perhaps a stockpile of basic slag.

There are the same messages to be read in the countryside, of course. Those long, thin bands of woodland in the limestone landscape of the Derbyshire Peak District are no accident. They are growing along the scars of ancient lead mining, where grass was always too contaminated to graze, sheep were walled out and the trees were allowed a chance to develop. The roads and lanes themselves still followed ancient routes, far older than the Romans; and the parallel stripes of medieval strip cultivation still give us ribbons of marsh-marigold in the damp troughs and drought-tolerant daisies on the crests. All these reminders of the past are fascinating, but in towns the past is so much nearer somehow. Old people can still remember the first cars and the days when the horse trough was as vital to the transport system as petrol pumps are today. Ask why a particular old building is the strange shape it is, or why there's a kink in the footpath, and no doubt someone will tell you.

The most strikingly obvious feature of any town or city is the buildings. They are the things that tell you it is a town, and perhaps not surprisingly, some species find buildings a major asset. Obviously the starlings and pigeons are well served by the roof tops, window sills and Gothic twiddly bits, and if you look carefully you will see that certain styles of building make much better roosts than others. A number of birds have adapted in recent years to nesting on and in buildings too. Swifts, house martins and swallows have a very long tradition of co-habiting with man. Swallows still tend to be restricted largely to farm buildings in the countryside, whilst swifts are very much town birds, favouring Gothic towers and spires wherever possible. House martins on the other hand are much more fond of new houses, often building their first nests whilst the windows are still unglazed and there is plenty of builder's mud around. This is rather unfortunate in a way, since they do make quite a mess, and the proud owner of a brand new 'Barratt's mock-Georgian' is probably going to be less than enthusiastic about a splattering of strong-smelling bird-droppings down bedroom windows and on the front doorstep. Maybe the builders should include a note with the sales documents, explaining that these beautiful little birds have flown 4000 miles, right across the Sahara, the Mediterranean and most of Europe, just to decorate that particular Tudor-glazed bedroom window. Perhaps then there would be fewer angry folks eager to knock the nests down.

All our native species of bats are seriously threatened and several are dangerously close to extinction. All are harmless; indeed, they are generally beneficial to man and although they have suffered from a very bad public image in the past, associated as they have been with vampires, werewolves and things that go bump in the night, they do seem gradually to be gaining in popularity. Some species of bat are hollow-tree

and cave-dwellers, and they have adapted to living in the
roof space of buildings, whilst others prefer cellars. The bigger
industrial cities still have relatively few colonies, since the
insect populations are only just recovering from the dark days
of heavy pollution, and even the tiny pipistrelle bat needs
about 3,000 insects per summer's night just to keep going.
In the smaller towns, though, bats are often present, and
when they are, they rely very heavily on buildings for roosting.
There is another advantage to urban living here, too. The
street lamps act as an irresistible magnet to night-flying insects.
Town-dwelling bats have quickly learned that a well-lit street
can provide a very fruitful hunting ground.

Bats and people have lived in reasonable harmony for
generations, no doubt generally oblivious of one another. In
fact, the bats do nothing but good in buildings – eating the
odd fly, beetle and spider that live in their roost, and even
providing extremely efficient heat insulation by spreading a
layer of their dry, non-smelling droppings over the loft floor.
Lately, though, the secret weapon of chemical warfare has
struck again. The growing use of unseasoned structural
timber, and the over-enthusiasm for air-tight roof spaces has
led to a boom in timber treatment. People have been sold
woodworm or dry rot prevention on a grand scale, and as the
lofts have been sprayed, colony after colony of beautiful,
harmless, precious bats has been exterminated. A combination
of this kind of roost damage, loss of insect food through
agricultural spraying, and a series of wet, cold summers has
led to a dramatic drop in bat populations – a reduction of
50% in six years for several species in the first half of the
1980s. Now, at last, there is very strong legislation to protect
them, timber treatment chemicals which do not harm bats are
available, and hopefully it isn't too late.

I mentioned town halls as good roosts for starlings and nest
sites for peregrines. They have a much more general role
to play too, in making town living more luxurious for wildlife.
A great deal of our urban green space is publicly owned,
and vast amounts of public money are spent managing it.
Parks and public open spaces are only a small part of the
public green. Add to them the schools, the hospitals, British
Rail land, gas board land, electricity board land, military,
drainage and waste disposal land, and you can see that
decisions in the town hall and the other public offices have a
great bearing on the quality of life in towns. The scale of this
public spending, even in periods of constraint, is still

enormous. The average hundred acre city park, for instance, will have a staff of four or five people at least, a garage full of machinery, and a budget for new planting each year. Where in the countryside could you find even one person per hundred acres available to manage the non-productive bits for public pleasure?

The huge amounts of public money are a mixed blessing. The cash tends to come in big lumps, that must be spent quickly. There is a preference for what is called 'capital spending' – buying things or changing things dramatically – rather than 'revenue spending', which might provide the 'little and often' funding needed for management. This means it is easier to find the money to clear an old existing landscape away and create a new one, than to care for the one that already exists, and so the cemeteries are tidied, the wild spoil heaps are levelled and the streams and rivers are straightened. In time I have no doubt society will come to its senses, and begin to use public money to employ people in caring for their environment, but for the time being, we can only try to steer the blitzkrieg of short-life, big-spend projects into areas where it can do least harm. There are times, too, when an injection of capital can benefit wildlife enormously. I remember working on a disused railway cutting, using derelict land grants to improve the landscape. A chunk of that cash was spent on a machine to block up the drainage, and create some very effective wetlands. There is often a need to build steps, give people safer access, put up the odd sign, or block off the route for fly-tippers. Certainly there is value in spending some money, but by and large, most public landscapes would benefit much more from a regular dose of caring, by officials who know the area and the folks who use it. This 'wardening' approach is practised with great success by some local authorities, but it is hard work making it fit the 'once and for all' public-spending straitjacket.

I've kept the biggest of the city-dweller wildlife benefits until last. That, of course, is the phenomenal supply of food which urban areas represent. Town wildlife benefits in three different ways. Firstly, there is the abundance of natural food present in our huge expanse of unsprayed wildspace. The richness of native wild plants feeds a wide range of creepy-crawlies and these in turn provide a rich food supply for higher animals.

Secondly, there is the food we throw away. Towns are very wasteful places. Not only do we allow our central heating to

It may be a load of rubbish to us, but to 'easy-to-please' scavengers, an upturned dustbin or a pile of refuse is just another happy hunting ground. This adventurous hedgehog is sure to find all kinds of delicious scraps amongst the cans and cartons – and if the slugs have found it first, so much the better. The hedgehog will gobble them up too.

leak out into the cold night air, warming the grateful pigeons; we also throw away vast mountains of edible waste every day. This is why the wildlife clean-up squad has done so well in towns. The fox is just the largest and most celebrated of our successful scavengers – prepared to eat pretty well anything. So long as you're not too choosy, the average British city is like a giant supermarket without a checkout. The birds feed by day, and so we are familiar with their antics as they hop on and off the pad of squashed chips beside the bus stop, or crane down inside the litter-basket to retrieve a half-eaten sandwich. The mammals tend mainly to operate by night, moving into the city centre as the last bus leaves for the suburbs, and they do a pretty thorough job, too. It is reasonable to assume that with so many tens of thousands of starlings roosting in towns, some, at least, would die, and drop off their window sills or fall from the trees each night. You never see any corpses, though. That is because the clean-up brigade has been there first. Even the busiest of city centres is on the circuit for some urban fox or another these days, and very little that can be eaten ever survives to see the light of day. With so many restaurant waste-bins, half-eaten take-away meals and wildlife road casualties around, the commonly held belief that foxes chase and kill cats is rather fanciful. That's too much like hard work.

Last but not least, there is all the food which kind, caring people like you and me put out specifically for the wildlife. I imagine the first hedgehog to discover a saucer of bread and milk must have fainted with shock. Those ducks and geese on the boating lake must be equally amazed to find that, after migrating two thousand miles to escape the frozen north, they are welcomed with handfuls of corn and crusts of bread. The birdtable is such a British institution that in many areas the limiting factor for populations of birds such as the blue tit is no longer food supply – it is that of finding enough holes in which to nest!

All in all, our towns and cities are a pretty good place to be if you are a fox or a bluetit, a peacock butterfly or a poppy. Many of the benefits are only there by accident, but it is possible to give more positive encouragement than that. Everyone can help, and if you have a garden, a corner of the school grounds, a hospital courtyard, or even a patch of wasteland you can adopt, then you can begin straight away by turning your own personal patch into a super service station for city wildlife.

MAPPING YOUR OWN NEIGHBOURHOOD HABITAT NETWORK

5

Wherever you live, whether it's in a city tower block or a rose-covered cottage in the countryside, there will be a definite pattern to the landscape around you. Some of your surroundings will be hostile to wildlife. At one extreme, this might be the field of wall-to-wall winter wheat, and at the other, the drab tarmac of the supermarket car park. In both cases there will be a network of places that are good for nature, too. Since the wildlife you can enjoy on your doorstep depends on that local neighbourhood habitat network, it obviously makes sense to find out more about it.

If you are lucky enough to have a garden with a buddleia bush in it, or a patch of buddleia-covered wasteland close to home, then I'm quite sure it's covered in small tortoiseshell and peacock butterflies in late summer. All these beautiful creatures must have spent the earlier part of their year as caterpillars, feeding on the leaves of stinging nettles somewhere close by, and once you begin looking, you will be able to put those two pieces of the jigsaw together. That kind of thing is interesting in its own right, but it can be critical, too, because a seemingly innocent 'tidy up' operation can so easily wipe out the nettle patch and with the best of intentions you can be robbed of your butterflies. Once you know how the neighbourhood ticks, then you can't help but try to save it, so as a first step towards the enjoyment and protection of wildlife in your area, I strongly recommend that you begin making notes about the local plants and animals, and the places where they live.

A neighbourhood habitat map can be enormously useful when it comes to helping wildlife. If a developer applies to

Once you begin to look properly, you are sure to discover a whole new landscape of wild green, unofficial places – the wild side of town. I spotted this patch from the local train, and a tour on a double-decker bus is very revealing too.

the council for permission to fill in a stream and build houses, you may be able to show that the stream in question is a vital link between the canal and the park lake, and the only reason why kingfishers manage to survive in your neighbourhood. That is a much more persuasive argument against the development than simply saying, 'It's a nice stream. Please don't spoil it.'

Your local neighbourhood habitat map is something you can start putting together any time, and, just as importantly, you will keep wanting to add to it as you spot more and more habitat detail. Sometimes you'll need to note a loss; as, for instance, when an old tree is felled to make way for a new house, but if that house has a garden, with a pond in it, then there is a new mini-habitat to add in for compensation, and what you have lost in songbirds and squirrels, your neighbourhood may gain in frogs and dragonflies.

The easiest way to begin is by letting your fingers do the walking, which is good news for armchair ecologists. The first step in drawing up your local neighbourhood habitat map is to look for the obvious network of green spaces on a map of the area, and then to go out and check on their quality as

habitats. The winter is a good time to start, when there is
less undergrowth and you can see further into private land.
In fact, I think it is a marvellous project for that lazy period
around Christmas. An evening by the fire poring over plans
followed by a vigorous safari in the fresh air of the following
morning, and then a de-briefing over a mince pie that same
evening – what could be better? You might even prefer to
split the tasks, with a housebound Granny or Grandpa
presiding over the maps at HQ, and energetic grandchildren
detailed to go off on voyages of discovery, to see if there really
is a stream along the back of the gasworks, or any signs of
fruit trees in Orchard Street.

In towns, the A–Z street-guide is quite a useful and cheap
map to use as a base. It certainly shows such things as
railways and rivers, as well as cemeteries, schools and parks.
In smaller towns and villages there won't be an A-Z, though
there could be a town map if it is a touristy sort of place. Don't
worry though, because as an alternative you can go straight
to the best maps of all. These are the several different scales
of map prepared by the Ordnance Survey. The ones that
are available most readily are the 1:50,000 scale maps. These
are the popular walker's 'one inch' maps. They've been
updated and metricated recently, but that makes no difference
so far as we are concerned. They cover big areas, and are
marvellous value for money, but they don't really give you a
great deal of detail once you move from the country areas

*A dismantled railway is an
obvious wildlife corridor. This
one in West Bromwich creeps in
its cutting for two and a half miles,
right through the town centre. It
is marked on my map as rich
wildspace.*

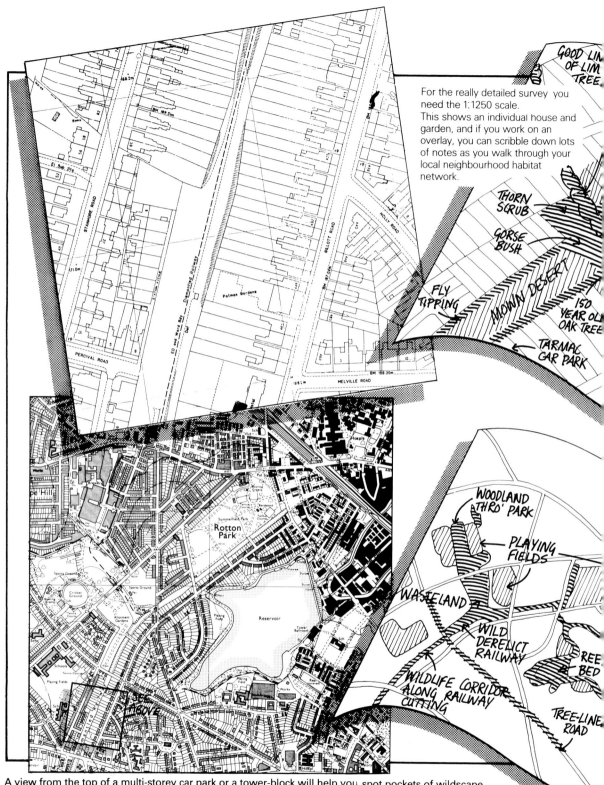

For the really detailed survey you need the 1:1250 scale.
This shows an individual house and garden, and if you work on an overlay, you can scribble down lots of notes as you walk through your local neighbourhood habitat network.

GOOD LINE OF LIME TREE

THORN SCRUB

GORSE BUSH

FLY TIPPING

MOWN DESERT

150 YEAR OLD OAK TREE

TARMAC CAR PARK

WOODLAND THRO' PARK

PLAYING FIELDS

WASTELAND

WILD DERELICT RAILWAY

REED BED

WILDLIFE CORRIDOR ALONG RAILWAY CUTTING

TREE-LINED ROAD

A view from the top of a multi-storey car park or a tower-block will help you spot pockets of wildscape which are hidden at ground level — and you can pick out the old hedgelines and other green corridors too.

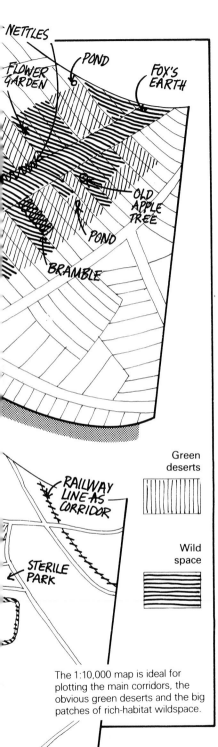

NETTLES

FLOWER GARDEN

POND

FOX'S EARTH

OLD APPLE TREE

POND

BRAMBLE

RAILWAY LINE AS CORRIDOR

STERILE PARK

Green deserts

Wild space

The 1:10,000 map is ideal for plotting the main corridors, the obvious green deserts and the big patches of rich-habitat wildspace.

into the towns. They will still show you where the wildlife corridors along the railways, rivers and canals are, and they will identify churches and schools, but only with a symbol.

The 1:25,000 scale is a bit better; it doesn't have as much colour on it, but you can pick out major open spaces more easily and it is very cheap. You will be able to get it through a good bookshop if you're prepared to wait a week or so. If you're near a big town with a branch of Her Majesty's Stationery Office, then you can buy one off the shelf. You will see that the map is divided up with thin black lines into squares. These each represent an area 1 kilometre, or 3/5ths of a mile, square, and I suggest you begin by surveying the kilometre square you live in. In the countryside this might represent the territory for a family of badgers, or a pair of kestrels. In the town, where the pickings are richer, you might have several families of foxes in a single square. If you choose to stick to the A-Z, then I suggest you survey the area covered by the page on which you live. That is a reasonable size of territory too.

The 1:25,000 is not really a large enough scale to use as a survey base. It's far too fiddly to put your notes on. There is a bigger version of the same map available from HMSO. In some areas it is the old 6-inches-to-the-mile, and in others, where the Ordnance Survey have updated things, the scale will be 1:10,000. At this scale all the individual houses and gardens are shown, and you really can begin to draw on individual trees and ponds, and put in the lines of hedgerows and so on. With modern photocopiers, you could blow up the plan to an even bigger scale, and that would make life easier still, but unfortunately, Ordnance Survey maps are protected by crown copyright, and you really need to seek permission, and then to pay a fee before you make any kind of copy. The 1:10,000 maps are very expensive, except in one or two towns where a cheap version called a 'City Map' has been published.

The Ordnance Survey publish one more, even larger scale map – the 1:1250 scale. This is big enough to make lots of notes on, and is the scale I use most, but each sheet covers a small area and the cost is high, so I usually lay a sheet of clear plastic over the map and make notes on that.

There is one more kind of 'map' which deserves a mention, and that is the aerial photograph. Towns in particular are photographed from the air quite frequently, and in many areas this is done by the local authority methodically every two or three years. In fact these days it is possible to take a snap from a satellite that will enable the experts to pick up details on the ground which are as small as a yard across. If you get in touch with the local council, and speak to the planning office or the surveyors, they may well allow you to pop in and take a look at the aerial photos of your neighbourhood, and perhaps even take away a black and white photocopy. With a bit of practice, you will be able to identify different vegetation types quite easily, as well as seeing just exactly what does go on in the back garden of number eight! If the council has coloured aerial photographs, then it is easier still, and you will be struck immediately by how green everywhere seems to be.

Well, that is enough about different bits of paper. It is foxes and hedgehogs, butterflies and bluetits we are really interested in, so you'll want to be rid of the paperwork as quickly as possible. Stage one of the survey can be done entirely from the comfort of your armchair, using the 1:10,000 map or the A–Z, and your existing knowledge of the area. I suggest you are looking for three elements in your local habitat network: 'corridors', 'green deserts', and 'wild space'. You are not really interested in the buildings and bits of tarmac in between – that is the dead ground so far as most of your local wildlife is concerned.

Look for the green deserts as well as the wildspace. This old industrial wasteland in County Durham is a marvellous tapestry of scrub woodland and unpolluted ponds – the only gaps are the close-mown municipal sports pitches in the middle.

Begin, then, by spreading a thin sheet of tracing paper over the map, or working on a photocopy if you can get one, and marking on these three elements as far as you can remember seeing them. Use two different greens – perhaps a bright green for the deserts, and a browner green for the wild space. Most of your corridors will be wild space, so they will mainly show up browny-green too, though there may well be stretches of desert where the engineers have 'improved' a stream or British Waterways Board have just dredged the canal.

Once you have your main network of major corridors and big green spaces marked up, you should start to look for the gaps. Think of yourself as a fox or hedgehog. Is there a way you can get from the canal corridor across to the railway cutting without having to break cover, or cross a busy road? If not, then you've got a corridor gap problem. Some of the gaps may well be green, of course, but there isn't much cover for a hedgehog crossing a football pitch.

You will quickly find that you need to go out and investigate on the ground. There may be a big factory blocking the corridor system, for instance, and you won't know if the boundary along the back of it is overgrown, leafy and green, or just a dull sheet of concrete and tarmac. If you have

Kingfishers don't fly down dark tunnels, so this culverted stream is a broken corridor. It is too late to save this particular wildlife link, but a good survey will help you argue for corridor protection against future threats.

managed to get hold of the aerial photograph, then that will tell you easily. If not, then there is no alternative, you just have to go out and look – and take the 1:1250 scale O.S. map with you.

Tall buildings are very useful when it comes to neighbourhood surveys. Even the simple measure of climbing up to higher ground will help you see the ribbons of green, and the hidden corners that lie behind the high walls and hedges. As you walk around your neighbourhood, or study the photographs and maps, you will build up more and more detail. You start to see that the major corridors have much smaller threads of green linking them; these include those ancient boundary hedgerows I talked about earlier, dividing pre-war and post-war housing estates, and sneaking across the bottom of back gardens. We have a section of one of these at the bottom of our garden, and it is a regular highway for grey squirrels, flocks of small birds and no doubt for hedgehogs and other more secretive wildlife, too. The suburban estate roads can also be important. They will not have the wild embankments of an urban motorway or a railway cutting, but there may be a central reservation, with a line of street trees along it, and this will help the birds to get around. There is a surprising number of streams and ditches trickling their way in secrecy throughout the suburbs. Most of them have been neglected, and they frequently disappear underground, where a road has been built, or over-intensive development has taken place. Nevertheless, they form a valuable complement to the bigger canals and rivers, and are often much more natural and rich in wildlife. Newts and frogs will breed here, and water voles, moorhens and even kingfishers will travel along them in some areas. Certainly they are a very important line of access to new garden ponds.

You will begin to spot pockets of land you hadn't noticed before. Suddenly the old demolished cinema is no longer a weed-covered eye-sore – it is another link in the chain of wildlife sites, rich in wildflowers, caterpillars and small mammals, rather than weeds, grubs and vermin. Keep adding to your map, and if there is a land-locked patch of neighbourhood that you simply can't see into, ask local people, the factory manager perhaps, or the householder with a bedroom window overlooking the hidden site. Who knows, in asking about it you may discover a valuable wildlife sanctuary and convert a new enthusiast into the bargain.

You will want to refine your first, simple map too. When you begin, it is convenient to write off the whole of the local recreation ground as 'green desert – ripe for improvement' and colour it in bright green. When you go and look at it you may well find that it actually has one or two really valuable features already. Although 95% of the area may be mown to death every ten days, you will probably find that there is a secluded corner somewhere where those grass-clippings are dumped; with so much 'compost' in one spot, this may well be the place where the nettles grow and your butterflies lay their eggs. Most of the trees in the local hospital grounds may be green desert lollipops, but there could well be a few big old stag-headed oaks there too, planted perhaps a hundred years ago, when the Victorian hospital was first built, and maybe providing a natural nesting site for a tawny owl or woodpecker.

With so much information to add to your map, you will need to develop a shorthand. You can use different colours of course – blue for water, and perhaps red or yellow for the weedy gap-sites. Those big old trees deserve a special symbol – and you might like to use a star system for the really important sites – two stars for the park lake, with its flocks of wild ducks in winter, and three stars for the overgrown cemetery, with its badger sett, its bat roost and its wild primroses.

The other aspect of your survey which is just as important as habitat mapping, is to start keeping records of the individual species of plants and animals that you find. You'll probably need a separate map for this, to avoid overcrowding, or if you're really clever you could use a system of map-references, and keep your wildlife records in a separate list. Divide your 1 km square into 100 small squares, with ten vertical columns and ten horizontal. Put numbers 1 to 10 across the top, and letters A–J down the side, and then you can pin-point your record to the nearest 100 metre square.

Entries such as 'Fox den in 7C' and 'Deadly nightshade in 3F' will be enough to remind you of precisely where they are. If you keep your records species by species, then over the years you can build up a picture showing just how common different species are. You'll perhaps have silver birch trees in seventy out of your hundred squares, but only ever see kestrels in the five squares where there is long grass for them to hunt over. If you manage to ring the changes, and the parks department develops a meadow, then you will probably start to see the kestrel there, too, and you will be able to show that the new habitat has helped at least one wild creature to extend its territory.

If you are a member of a group – say a school class or a branch of the RSPB – you can have a lot of people each surveying their own little patch, and then piece the bits together to make a much bigger network survey. A combined effort like this gives you more clout when you're locked in a battle to save a site, too. In 1982, and again in 1983, the Urban Wildlife Group organised just such a habitat survey in Birmingham. Each volunteer was asked to survey the area covered by one page of the A–Z and the amount of information that resulted was amazing. Over four hundred people joined in the first survey, and between them they discovered lots of interesting wildlife sites, enjoyed meeting one another to exchange 'data' and of course they also found a great deal out about their own area.

Once you have a picture of the way your neighbourhood works, and the kind of wildlife that lives there, you can get great enjoyment out of seeing how your own particular little patch links in to the rest of your surroundings. As the bluetits feed on the peanuts outside the classroom window, schoolchildren can try to work out where the hole might be in which these pretty little birds will nest next spring – it could be one of the big old trees in the school grounds, a hole in the old brick wall at the back of the railway station, or possibly one of the nest-boxes the woodwork class have made and fixed up on the school itself. When the hedgehog turns up with her family of soft-spined little piglets, to snuffle and splash their way through the nightly saucer of bread and milk, your family can try to work out which route they followed, where the babies were born, and which pile of leaves and logs they will choose to bury themselves in for hibernation next winter. Gradually you will begin to realise that the animals you see and enjoy, whether they are butterflies on the garden flowers, tits on the bird-table, or a fox you only see fleetingly in the car headlights, all depend on a complex network of habitats. Once you understand the way your neighbourbood ticks, you can start to help the habitats survive, and you will have some really good clues to the kind of wildlife it's worth trying to attract into your own private garden, your tower block window sill or the space outside your office or classroom. You can aim to provide the perfect service station for all those animals and plants that are busy making a living in your locality.

Get in early with your survey, and new developments can be forced to take account of the wildlife network. This old hedgeline could so easily have been built on. Instead it has been carefully retained, and now it forms an attractive feature of the new housing estate, bringing hedgehogs, song-birds and many other wild creatures right into the back gardens.

MAKING A WILDLIFE SUPER SERVICE STATION GARDEN

6

When I left school and started work as a parks' trainee in Sheffield, one of my first jobs was with the mobile gang that cared for the traffic islands, the flower-beds in the town hall gardens, and the various tubs of flowers around the city centre. It was World Cup year and I had the dubious honour of being allowed to water the dozens of flower baskets which hung from the lamp posts in the High Street. This privilege involved rising at 5 am and wobbling my way from basket to basket, perched on top of a step-ladder on the back of a lorry.

I very quickly learned that our daily routine, and particularly the circuit we followed from flower-bed to traffic island to war memorial, was determined by food and drink, and so entirely structured to take in all the best cafés in our patch. As you might expect, your wandering city wildlife also aims to include the best stopping-off points for food and drink. Our famous fox will make a nightly call at several particularly

Caught in the act. This young fox was visiting my garden for an early morning drink at the pond, before finding a safe, overgrown corner in which to sleep out the day.

productive kitchen dustbins. Most hedgehogs will know of a damp spot where there are always snails and slugs to be found. The greater-spotted woodpecker will return time and time again to the same sickly silver birch tree, because the wood is soft, and there are always lots of larvae there to be dug out. Kestrels and owls will move methodically from one patch of rough grass to the next, simply because that is where they are most likely to find food. Even butterflies will travel miles on a summer's day, only stopping to feed on flowers with plenty of nectar, and flowers the right shape for them to land on and feed from.

When you see the spectacular setting of a Sunday night in the Serengeti, or the Amazon jungle, courtesy of BBC 2, you must have wondered, like me, how the camera always seems to be in just the right place for those wonderful close-up shots of shy animals. The answer is simple. Those landscapes, like every other, have their sprinkling of watering holes and feeding places – wildlife service stations. Provide the water, or the carcass of a poor unfortunate goat, set up your camera, sit back and wait for the wildlife to come to you.

Now I can't promise you a pride of lions or wallowing warthogs outside your kitchen window, but if you follow the same principle, providing a rich variety of foods, fresh water and, of course, some care and protection, then even in the tiniest patch, in the heart of the city, you can expect to see more than your fair share of visiting wildlife. You don't necessarily need your own garden either. Any safe corner of land will do. The essential ingredient for a successful service station is that the food must be good, and that the supply must be reliable. The most amazing bird-feeding I ever saw took place in a park on the edge of Amsterdam. I watched, open-mouthed, as a little old man was 'mobbed' by an astonishing variety of birds. Robins and bluetits were feeding out of his hand. There is nothing remarkable about that of course – you can see it in most British parks. The difference here was that this man had jays fetching acorns, coaltits collecting peanuts, and most astonishing of all, wild herons cautiously stretching their necks towards him and snatching lumps of boiled ham. I was with the park's superintendent at the time, and he explained that this old gentleman visited the same spot every day, had built up the confidence of the wildlife, and knew exactly which food each species liked best.

It is probably best to start your own service station with a bird-table. Our wild birds are very mobile, obviously; they

OPPOSITE: Provide a variety of foods – both soft and hard. Always make sure there is clean water for drinking and bathing, and remember that some birds prefer to feed on the ground.

are colourful and entertaining, and they respond very quickly to a new source of food. A table is a good idea because it gives the birds a sense of security by ensuring that they have good all-round visibility, and it can be placed exactly where you too can have the best view.

Choose a spot for your 'bird feeding station' which is close to a window. The birds will learn to disregard the movements on the other side of the glass, and you can watch in comfort. It is useful to have it close to the building for another reason too. Once you begin feeding you must keep it up absolutely religiously. The birds will quickly come to rely on you. Give yourself a hundred yard trek to the bird-table and even the keenest of conservationists will probably chicken out on the very morning when the snow is thickest and the birds are most in need of your help.

Ideally, the feeding should take place in an open patch, with a tree or a shrub or two just a short flight away, but without too much cat-cover within pouncing distance. The table itself must be solid, fixed firmly to a post, and at least five feet high. There should be a vertical upstand around the edge, just half an inch or so high, to help stop the food blowing off, and gaps in this surround to allow rainwater to drain away. A roof is quite a good idea, as it keeps the food dry, and does keep the very big birds off, but it is certainly not essential. A few hooks, or nails, around the edge will enable you to hang food there for the more acrobatic birds. A good idea is to make a dish-sized hole for a drinking-water bowl, so that

this can't blow away, and I certainly recommend you drill a small hole in one corner of your table and wedge in a branching twig. This provides a 'stepping stone' for the more cautious birds, and somewhere for the queue to form when your table becomes really popular.

You will get the best results if you feed at the same time each day. The birds are most in need of help first thing in the morning, when their energy reserves are low after a long cold night. Try putting their breakfast out before you have yours, then you can have a race to see who finishes first.

Different species eat different kinds of food, so variety is the spice of life. Provide a mixture of soft foods such as fat, cheese and fruit, and hard seeds too. Specialist suppliers such as John Haith and Son of Cleethorpes offer various mixtures, and I usually treat my birds to a big bag of the soft-bill mixture, and another of hard-bill seed-mix each winter. If you feed bread, then it is worth remembering that over-purified white bread is as bad for the birds as it is for humans. Choose a wholemeal loaf 'with nowt tecken out' for preference – but don't be silly about it. White bread is very much better than nothing at all. The one thing you must avoid is salted peanuts. They really are killers.

What I try to do is beg a bag of fat-scraps from my long-suffering local butcher Mr Harris each weekend. I fill the house with the eyewatering smell of burning as I melt the fat down, and then I mix the molten fat with the various other foods I have available. Bits of bread, seed, cheese and fruit all go into the bowl. When it is thoroughly mixed, I put it somewhere cool to set. It then gets tipped out as one solid lump, and is reduced to nothing by eager beaks over the next few days.

I have a plastic seed-hopper on a stick for the sparrows. This keeps the seed dry, and is constantly attended by a ring of five sparrows, pecking away for all the world like one of those Russian toys made of wood, with pecking chickens brought to life by a swinging ball.

The small, more agile birds are able to feed from bags or strings of nuts, hung on the side of the table. There was a time when these were the exclusive domain of the bluetits, but each year the list of accomplished acrobats grows longer. The red plastic nets seem to be the most attractive, and probably the easiest to cling to. So far in our garden we've been entertained by great tits, coal tits, marsh tits, greenfinches, house sparrows, a greater spotted and a lesser

Every wildlife service station needs a bird-feeder. Bluetits may be the first to discover your peanuts, but by the middle of a hard winter they could be competing with a dozen other acrobatic species.

spotted woodpecker and a starling. If you have a wood nearby, you may even be visited by nuthatches. Our latest recruits are a small flock of siskins. These handsome little birds look for all the world like slim-line greenfinches, but the male has a sooty cap. They breed in the forests of Scandinavia and northern Scotland, and fly south in their thousands, to escape the winter, and feed in mixed flocks with redpoll and long-tailed tits. Their favourite food in the wild is alder seed, and that presumably is how they became natural acrobats, hanging upside down on the springy twigs of riverbank alder trees. For the ten or so in my personal flock, peanuts in red plastic bags have replaced alder as their staple diet.

I find it particularly thrilling to know that my care in the winter is really making a genuine contribution to international nature conservation. The folk that feed the birds in their gardens are responsible for saving the lives of tens of thousands of our winter migrants each year. If only we could be equally conscientious as a nation about the pollution we produce. Remember that our power stations and car exhausts are helping create the acid rain that drifts across the North Sea and kills the forests that are the siskins' summer breeding-grounds.

Some species you are likely to attract to your service station will be very wary about feeding up in the air on a bird-table. Blackbirds and songthrushes will oblige if pushed, but they are very nervous. That beautiful little bird, the dunnock, or hedge sparrow, is much too shy, and generally prefers to hop around on the ground below, picking up the debris scattered by your extrovert starlings. The wren is another secretive feeder, and so, surprisingly, is the otherwise cheeky chaffinch. For this reason I generally try to provide some food on the open ground, and for much of the winter this is simply a matter of throwing a handful of rotting apples on to the back lawn. If the snow falls, then the birds move in by the dozen, and you can be pretty sure that, sooner or later, the redwings and fieldfares will join in. These beautiful foreign thrushes are two more species of seasonal refugees from the frozen north. They cross the North Sea in huge flocks, and concentrate on hawthorn berries up until Christmas. Once the year has turned, and natural food is running low, they gather in their hundreds on the local football pitch, heads to the wind and motionless. When the apples hit the frozen lawn, in they come. Although they are always lumped together – redwings and fieldfares – they really are very different.

The redwing looks like a cross between a songthrush and a robin, and is a shy, gentle bird. By contrast, the fieldfare is even bigger than a mistle thrush, with a handsome grey and chestnut plumage, and is a really aggressive bully. I've watched a dozen patient redwings sit in what looks for all the world like embarrassed silence around the garden, whilst their shameless fellow Scandinavian fieldfare friend flaps and thrusts its way around the lawn, driving away blackbirds, starlings and anything else that dares to covet a beakful of rotten apple. This is really rather strange behaviour, given the obvious abundance of food, and the energy such aggession must waste. Inevitably in the end, the other birds begin to call the fieldfare's bluff, and meet each offensive with the bird equivalent of a withering look.

Hygiene is quite important when considering a feeding area. It is advisable to move the bird-table every few seasons, to avoid the risk of a build-up of bird diseases, and on a day-to-day basis you must try to avoid accumulating old food. It may be tempting to pile the bird-table high with turkey remains after Christmas, but unless you have the equivalent of a vulture tribe living in the area, the feast is likely to sit there festering for days. The smell of this kind of thing may at best attract the attention of the local fox, who could well demolish the bird-table in its eagerness to run off with the booty. At worst it will attract less welcome visitors. The local cats will start to include you in their territorial night-time circuit, and you may even begin to attract rats. If food isn't cleared within a day or two, the best thing to do is remove it and put out a smaller portion of something more appetising.

Buying all this special food is expensive, and there is also the moral question of whether importing seedcrops from the Third World to feed the wild birds of Britain is really a wise use of the earth's resources. As an alternative you can, of course, grow your own, or collect it from the wild. If you are a country wine-maker, save the elderberry seeds and bramble pips for mixing into the bird pudding. Collect acorns and hawthorn berries in the early autumn. Dry them and dole them out to the birds when times get hard. If you have room, either in your garden or on your adopted wasteplot, there are lots of lovely plants to grow which will produce seeds for the birds, and you won't even have to venture outside on icy mornings.

Every wildlife service station should have sunflowers growing in it. If you can get the seedlings off to an early

When the hawthorn berries run out, blackbirds like this one will quickly join song and mistle thrushes, redwings and fieldfares, and strip the berries from pyracantha, cotoneaster and holly in the wildlife garden service station.

start, and give them a bucket or two of water now and then, you can expect those tiny little black and white striped seeds to perform a miracle for you, and leap nine or ten feet in the air by July. Leave the flowers till the autumn, and if there is anything like a reasonable summer, you can expect their big, brown faces to be bulging with thousands of seeds.

The birds will find them soon enough. Greenfinches and great tits are particularly fond of them. If you want the crop to survive until the colder weather, then cut the stems once they are ripe, and hang them upside down somewhere dry until the time is right. If you don't have much growing space, if your patch is vulnerable to vandals, or you are afraid the wind will topple your giants, I suggest you nip out the top when the seedlings are about eighteen inches tall. Side branches will then form and you should have four or five saucer-sized blooms per plant instead of one giant soup-plate.

The teasel is another flower worth growing for its seed. Sunflowers are annuals, and flower and fruit in the first year. Teasels are biennials, and wait until their second season before thrusting up their two-metre high candelabra of prickly purple flowers. The seed is not particularly big, but it seems to be very tasty. The sharp spines of the brown seedhead protect the seed very effectively, but one species of finch has a specially adapted face, ideal for delving deep in among the spines and teasing out the teasel seed. That bird is the goldfinch, perhaps the most brightly coloured of all our wild species, and the patch of red feathers on its face is especially toughened. I guarantee that if you grow teasels, and let them run to seed, then at some time in November a tinkling charm of goldfinches will descend on them and devour the lot. In fact, the relationship between teasels and goldfinches is so predictable, that illegal bird-trappers used the seed heads to lure goldfinches down into their traps.

Blackbirds and the various species of thrush basically eat berries. They can't crack seeds, and in cold weather there are no worms near enough to the lawn's surface to be dragged out. In the wild, hawthorn, sloe and rosehip are the major food of winter, but in your service station you can grow a whole range of more exotic fruiting species. If you are feeling generous, then raspberries, redcurrants and blackcurrants seem pretty popular, but assuming that you fancy those for yourself, try planting some of the cotoneasters and pyracanthas instead. These are exotic relatives of the hawthorn, and they

Garden flowers can extend the nectar season for butterflies. Here a small tortoiseshell, newly emerged from hibernation, is feeding on my grape hyacinth flowers in early March.

<table>

</table>

NECTAR FLOWERS

for butterflies, moths and
other useful insects

Christmas rose	*Helleborus niger*
Winter aconite	*Eranthis hyemalis*
Elephant's ears	*Bergenia cordifolia*
Spring crocus	*Crocus chrysanthus* and hybrids
Anemone	*Anemone blanda*
Grape hyacinth	*Muscari botryoides*
Lenten rose	*Helleborus orientalis*
Polyanthus	*Primula vulgaris elatior*
Soldiers and sailors	*Pulmonaria saccharata*
White arabis (single)	*Arabis albida*
Honesty	*Lunaria biennis*
Sweet rocket	*Hesperis matronalis*
Aubretia	*Aubretia deltoidea*
Wallflower	*Cheiranthus cheiri*
Forget-me-not	*Myosotis* spp
Leopard's bane	*Doronicum pardalianches*
Golden alyssum	*Alyssum saxatile*
Sweet William	*Dianthus barbatus*
Perennial cornflower	*Centaurea montana*
Poached egg plant	*Limnanthes douglasii*
Shasta daisy	*Chrysanthemum maximum*
Fleabane	*Erigeron speciosus* varieties
Cranesbills	*Geranium* species
Sweet bergamot	*Monarda didyma*
Evening primrose	*Oenothera biennis*
Oriental poppy	*Papaver orientale*

Continued

fruit very heavily indeed. Elderberry is particularly popular with starlings, but fruits rather early in the autumn, before there is any real risk of starvation, and as I have already said, apples are a guaranteed success if you leave them uneaten for long enough.

Use my list by all means, but the best way of discovering new plants for the service station is by observation. Redwings and blackbirds strip the berries from my variegated holly each year, but not until after Christmas. How considerate! Bullfinches have a weakness for the papery seedheads of honesty, and for dandelion clocks, too. Golden rod attracts the sparrows, but they seem to need to rediscover it every year.

This technique of looking and learning is also invaluable when you are choosing nectar and pollen plants. If birds provide your wildlife entertainment in the cold of winter, then in summer it is insects that provide the show. The measure of any wildlife habitat is the health and abundance of its invertebrate population, and a good wildlife garden should be buzzing in the summer. Butterflies are the glamorous members of the group, and certainly we do have a wonderfully colourful selection, though most are in rapid decline, and several species are close to extinction. There are about a dozen species that you can expect to see in the middle of town, with the range reducing as you travel north, and certainly a 'gap-site' or a sheltered courtyard can make a marvellous 'butterfly-pub' as Miriam Rothschild calls it. Butterflies drink nectar, and if you provide an ample supply through the whole length of the spring, summer and early autumn, then you can't really fail. Of course there are good years and bad years. Long weeks of cold and rain will reduce numbers dramatically. If we have a hot, dry June and a strong southerly wind, then all kinds of unexpected rarities such as clouded yellows are blown over from the Continent, but by and large, a well-planted butterfly border can expect to attract orange-tip, brimstone, painted lady, small tortoiseshell, peacock, red admiral, comma, speckled wood, common blue, large white and small white.

For the best effect you need a sequence of suitable flowers, beginning with grape hyacinth in March, and ending with ice-plant, Michaelmas daisy and ivy in October. Flowers which are simple in shape and easy to land on are generally better than more complicated ones. Snapdragons, for instance, are hopeless for butterflies. There are a number of annuals which I find especially good. Candytuft is like a magnet to a whole range of species. Mauve and purple flowers tend to work particularly well, so lavender, honesty and purple loose-strife never fail, and, of course, the star of the butterfly border is the good old buddleia. Again the flowers tend to be purples and mauves, though white varieties seem to work just as well. Put your nose close to the flower and you are left in no doubt as to the reason for its attractiveness. Every spray of buddleia smells as if it has been freshly dipped in honey. *Buddleia Davidii* is a shrubby pioneer of rubbly soils in its native China, and it has romped away to form huge colonies on many of our city demolition sites. With a bright green band of stinging nettles along the roadside, vigorously growing with their roots in the nitrogen-rich piles of fly-tipped garbage, and a forest of sweet-smelling buddleia bushes beyond, the peacocks and small tortoiseshells must think they are in heaven.

Butterflies aren't the only interesting insects one can find in towns – far from it. They do seem to get most of the publicity, but there are thousands of other species which, though less flamboyant, can be every bit as rewarding if you take the trouble to watch them. Most of them feed on pollen and nectar, though of course there are others that chew away at rotten wood, or suck the sap from leaves and stems, and of course there are some, like the dragonflies, that are predators and feed on other insects. Extend the range of flowers and you will extend the variety of insect visitors you attract. Bees can pollinate many kinds of flowers, and there are numerous species of bee, too, but they seem to have exclusive rights to the pollen and nectar of the bigger pea-type flowers. It takes an insect with the weight of a bumblebee to lever the flowers jaws open, and then the compact shape of a bee to crawl deep inside and still be able to turn round and escape. Grow a patch of snapdragons or broad beans in your service station and you will see what I mean.

Another group of fascinating insects that deserves a mention are the hoverflies. These little black and yellow 'rugby players' seem to prefer yellow flowers and white flowers, so I always grow marigolds, Californian poppies and golden rod. In recent years I have discovered another marvellous hoverfly magnet too. I leave one or two carrots in my veg patch over winter, and the following summer they send up beautiful fronds of fern-like leaves, and great umbrellas of brilliant white flowers. The hoverflies love them, and I've counted as many as twenty on a single cluster.

NECTAR FLOWERS

for butterflies, moths and other useful insects

Spiked speedwell	*Veronica spicata*
Valerian	*Centranthus ruber*
Sweet alyssum	*Alyssum maritimum*
Angelica	*Angelica archangelica*
Lovage	*Levisticum officinale*
Tobacco plant	*Nicotiana affinis*
Mignonette	*Reseda odorata*
Corncockle	*Agrostemma githago*
Yarrow	*Achillea millefolium*
Alkanet	*Anchusa officinalis*
Chicory	*Cichorium intybus*
Yellow loosestrife	
	Lysimachia vulgaris
Hollyhock	*Althaea rosea*
Snapdragon	*Antirrhinum majus*
Candytuft	*Iberis umbellata*
Californian poppy	
	Eschscholtzia californica
Sunflower	*Helianthus annuus*
Mallow	*Lavatera rosea*
Golden rod	*Solidago canadensis*
Phlox	*Phlox paniculata*
Teasel	*Dipsacus fullonum*
Basil	*Ocimum basilicum*
Mint	*Mentha spicata*
Globe thistle	*Echinops ritro*
Meadow saffron	
	Colchicum autumnale
Cosmos	*Cosmea bipinnatus*
Cherry pie	*Heliotropium x hybridum*
Michaelmas daisy	
	Aster amellus, A. acris, A. novae angliae, A. novi belgii

Continued

NECTAR FLOWERS

for butterflies, moths and other useful insects

Ice plant	*Sedum spectabile*
Annual woodruff	
	Asperula azurea setosima
Annual scabious	
	Scabiosa atropurpurea
Night-scented stock	
	Matthiola bicornis
Ageratum	*Ageratum houstonianum*
Ivy	*Hedera helix*
Sea holly	*Eryngium maritimum*
Cuckoo flower *or* milkmaids	
	Cardamine pratensis
Knapweed	*Centaurea nigra*
Hemp agrimony	
	Eupatorium cannabinum
Water mint	*Mentha aquatica*
Winter heliotrope	*Petasites fragrans*
Dandelion	*Taraxacum officinale*
Verbena	*Verbena officinalis*
Butterfly bush	*Buddleia davidii*
Weeping butterfly bush	
	Buddleia alterifolia
Clerodendrum	
	Clerodendrum trichotomum
Privet	*Ligustrum ovalifolium*
Shrubby veronicas	*Hebe* spp
Thyme	*Thymus* spp
Lavender	*Lavandula spica*
Bramble	*Rubus fruticosus*
Glory of the snow	*Chionodoxa luciliae*
Tansy	*Tanacetum vulgare*
Convolvulus	*Convolvulus tricolor*
Hedge woundwort	*Stachys sylvatica*
Marjoram	*Origanum vulgare*

That is the birds and bees catered for, but what everyone yearns for, it seems, is their very own visiting hedgehog. If all you have is a window-box on the tenth floor, then you could be in trouble, but apart from high-rise dwellers, most people are already sharing their neighbourhood with a family of hedgehogs. After all, a recent survey by the *Observer* newspaper's Young Naturalists Club suggests that a staggering one and a quarter million are killed on the roads each year, so there must be huge populations, lurking out there somewhere. Hedgehogs are very noisy, but only when they are feeding, or avoiding one another's prickles in the mating season. When they are on the move they are very fast, and generally silent. So if you live in a 'desert zone' you can be excused for thinking there are no local hedgehogs at all.

They are there, in fact, but they are nipping straight through your patch like high-speed clockwork broom-heads, hellbent on getting to the next service station. What hedgehogs really love are slugs and snails. They will eat almost anything, from carrion (another reason you never see dead birds) to bread and milk, but top of the menu is slugs. This makes them very valuable to gardeners and very vulnerable to garden chemicals, too, of course. If they regularly visit a veg patch where the slugs are dosed with poison, then pretty soon your snuffly friends will snuff it. If you want a healthy hedgehog, then you must provide a chemical-free zone, with plenty of cover in the flower borders or the shrubberies, and a reasonable degree of untidiness to satisfy the slugs. Bread and milk is really no substitute, and can even be harmful if it forms too large a part of the diet. A saucer of chopped meat would be better, or if you are really keen you could gather the slugs yourself, and leave them in a spot where you can watch. On second thoughts, the idea of a nature lover serving up sacrificial slugs just to secure a little armchair entertainment is a bit barbaric. It is much more fun to creep outside on a muggy June evening, torch in hand, and listen for the grunting and snuffling that will lead you to the feeding grounds of this very special wild creature.

Once you have hedgehogs visiting you regularly, you should give some thought to providing a hibernation habitat for them. I'll deal with habitat creation in much more detail later, but in the case of the hedgehog, you can kill two birds with one stone. Create a nice big pile of dead logs, fallen leaves and compost in a quiet corner of the garden, and your little friend will hunt slugs and snails there through the summer, and is quite likely to crawl inside and curl up for the winter, too.

So far I have only talked about the food aspect of wildlife service stations. Water is every bit as important, and indeed at certain times of year and in certain localities it may be a much rarer commodity. The rarer it is, the more likely you are to pull in the punters. If you can afford the luxury of a pond, then it will provide you with endless entertainment and contribute enormously to the local wildlife network. The one in my garden is visited regularly by dozens of birds, splashing and squawking in the shallows. Whatever else you do, though, you must provide a regular supply of clean drinking water along with your winter bird food. This should be in a shallow dish with a perchable rim, and it will need checking every morning. The messier feeders tend to pollute the water with bits of food, and of course on really cold nights the water will freeze. That is the moment when drinking water becomes critical to survival, and yours may be the only supply. Don't be tempted to add anti-freeze. I know you would never do anything so stupid, but it does happen, and of course it poisons the birds. If you are unable to check the water for some reason, there are a couple of ways of solving the freeze-up problem. Some people put their water dish over

A safe bathing site is a real life-saver for small birds in winter. Clean feathers make better, fluffier insulation – vital on frosty nights.

a night light, and the gentle heat keeps the ice away. As an alternative you can set up an insulated drinking trough by wrapping a big plastic pop-bottle filled with water in an old woolly jumper, and fixing it upside-down with its neck submerged in a shallow bowl. The insulation keeps it from freezing and water is gradually released as the wild birds and animals drink.

In the most sophisticated service stations, you can take a shower before you continue your journey. For a long-distance lorry driver this may just be a comfort stop. For wild birds the business of bathing is a matter of life and death, so do try and offer bathing facilities in your wildlife service station if you can. You need a shallow container, with gently sloping sides. An upturned dustbin lid is ideal, and if you set it on a square of bricks you can slide a small oil lamp underneath it on frosty evenings. Birds keep warm by fluffing up their feathers, and to do this efficiently they must be very clean. In the short days of winter, feeding must be the first priority, and there is little time for preening. A really good splash in shallow clean water is just the job, and every afternoon, about an hour before dark, you will see dozens of birds splashing away, freshening up their feathers to face another freezing night.

The final feature of a five-star service station is overnight shelter, or daytime shelter if you are nocturnal. Plenty of cover is a great attraction. So far as birds are concerned, those evergreen trees and shrubs that feature in so many British gardens are a godsend. What better place to settle down for the night, than deep in the heart of a leyland cypress or a holly bush. Nestle in behind the ivy on the wall of a building and you have near perfection, with the warmth of the building trapped behind the insulating layer of leaves. I've only very recently discovered that the house itself is a very popular night-time roost. Stand very still, below the eaves, just as darkness falls, and you will witness a most amazing thing. One after another, small birds will flutter silently under the overhang of the roof, and disappear. My particular home extension was blessed with a hopeless builder who left bricks out, and gaps in the woodwork everywhere. The birds couldn't be more pleased. A dozen or more of my feathered friends occupy those little nooks and crannies every night, and emerge warm and lively the morning after, eager to see what goodies 'muggins' has put out for them on his super-service-station running buffet.

RUBBLE AND RATS

7

People are constantly surprised that a garden designed for wildlife can be so colourful and orderly. They seem to expect a great patch of overgrown weeds. In fact, you only begin to get really troublesome weeds when you cultivate the soil. As soon as you hoe your shrub-borders, or fork over the vegetable patch, you prepare a seed bed. Dormant seeds in the soil are joined by the invaders that arrive by parachute. Their combined forces cover the ground with 'weeds' while your back's turned.

Of course 'weeds' are only a problem if they are growing in the wrong place. What more beautiful sight could there possibly be than a cornfield full of poppies – unless you are a farmer and it is your cornfield. The rich variety of weeds that quickly colonise disturbed ground are of great natural history value in themselves, and many of them are now extremely rare, particularly where farmers and gardeners use herbicides. These plants are also the life support system for a huge variety of animals. It is worth remembering that many of the invertebrates – the humble wriggly things and creepy crawlies – are terribly choosy about what they themselves eat. Many of the grubs and caterpillars you might find on an average weed-patch are munching the leaves of the only species of plant that they can live on. Their food requirements are absolutely specific. Most people know, for instance, that peacock butterflies must have young nettle shoots to lay their eggs on. That is because the spiky black caterpillars that emerge are unable to eat any other kind of plant. Native wild animals like the butterflies and moths are almost always dependent on native plants. That isn't surprising if you think about it. Our native wildlife communities have evolved over thousands of years, and they are bound to have become closely interdependent. A weed patch is a diverse collection of native plants, and consequently it will support a richer

As rubbish rots down, it boosts the soil's fertility, and sheets of stinging nettles often spring up. Young children know the value of these plants . . .

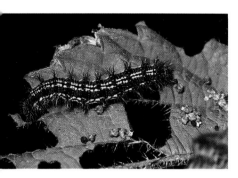

. . . as larval food for the caterpillars of such colourful butterflies as the small tortoiseshell.

than average variety of invertebrates. That piece of information is particularly significant in two ways. Firstly, if you are trying to increase wildlife populations, and especially the range of different kinds of wildlife, it is obviously best to grow native plants. Secondly, it makes a nonsense of the idea that the caterpillars in the weed patch down the road are likely to nip over the fence at dead of night, and devour the 'proper plants' growing in respectable gardens. The opposite is true. The only caterpillars likely to eat your cabbages, for instance, are those of the large and small cabbage white butterflies. They will be quite uncommon in a weed patch, since they themselves are so choosy about the leaves they eat. The cabbages in the neighbour's vegetable garden are an infinitely greater threat as a source of infection for the 'proper' garden. In fact, an adjacent weed patch is likely to do more good than harm to its neighbours. The abundance of native plants generates a healthy population of plant-eating invertebrates, and a feast like this will attract and support an equally vigorous population of predators. Given half a chance, it is the predators, rather than the 'pests', which hop over the fence, and knock off your neighbour's slugs and caterpillars.

If you have room in your garden, I think it is worth cultivating a patch of 'weeds' each year, and seeing just what a rich variety of both plants and animals appear. If that sounds a bit too crazy, then look around for a patch of wasteground, and have a dabble there. The most colourful 'weeds' do best on poorer ground, so don't feel you need to offer them a pocket of rich loam. That is the last thing you want. It will just produce a clump of vigorous, aggressive, dull weeds such as fat hen and chickweed, and you will wish you had never listened to me. I have grown 'weeds' on a small scale at Pebble Mill, on a part of my little wildlife garden in the studio grounds. The weed patch was made by raking over a patch of crushed tarmac and gravel with no soil in it at all. To speed up the process, and make sure I had plenty of colourful flowers, I sowed the area very thinly with a packet of mixed cornfield weeds. These are sometimes sold as 'Farmers' nightmare' in garden centres and they include such pretty, and increasingly rare, species as corncockle, pheasant eye, corn marigold, scentless mayweed, cornflower, heartsease, charlock and the inevitable field poppy. A sowing in April produces a brilliant display by midsummer, and I think this is the simplest way to persuade people that wildlife can be fun. You can keep a colony of these wildflowers going

for several years, provided you shake off the seeds in early autumn, and stir up the surface before the following spring.

The garden annuals we all grew as children are, of course, simply the 'cornfield weeds' from another part of the world. Grown here their leaves support very few of our native mini-beasts, but the flower colour is often brighter, and it is not a bad idea to mix in a few seeds to add even more variety. I would suggest you try Virginia stock, candytuft, Californian poppy and calendula, since they are particularly easy to grow, and they won't swamp your native annuals.

As I keep on saying, weedy urban gap-sites make marvellous wildlife habitat – the trouble is they have a terrible image which attracts abuse.

The simplest, and most effective way of reducing fly-tipping, is to tidy up the edges. A six foot verge of neatly-mown grass will act like a magic circle – firmly establishing your wasteland as an official, cared-for place. Once you decide to adopt your wasteland site, it pays dividends if you can make a real effort to remove rubbish which does still appear. Keep the site edges clear for a few weeks, and the pattern of abuse will be broken.

Another simple device which seems to work is to give the site a name, and label it. People seem much more able to accept and respect a site if it is no longer anonymous. Beware, though. Do try to avoid signs which are too smart, or which sound terribly official. Talk of large fines and prosecution will

Poppies need disturbance. Some of our most colourful wild species thrive on upheaval. The weeds of cultivation – thistles, teasels, white campion and corncockle - all need open ground for germination, and they quickly attract butterflies, and seed-eating finches, too.

Some of our best nectar-plants grow on rubble sites. Thistles, the farmer's nightmare, score ten out of ten as wildlife plants. Here a beautiful peacock butterfly adds a touch of exotic glamour to a wayside dump.

A simple sign and a neat edge make wasteland respectable

Brambles and other climbers cover the piles of junk

WILDLIFE LIVES HERE.

Use spare stones and bricks to build a low, double-sided boundary wall

meet with the response it deserves, and your sign will quickly be added to the piles of rubbish you are trying to reduce. A simple sign, *asking* people to take care of the site, or simply teaching them that 'Wildlife lives here' is much more likely to survive. When I first started work on a gap-site in Brixton, the children painted a board which explained that this was a place they cared about. On an estate where official signs rarely survived a week, this one was left unmolested for several years.

Although dumped rubbish is the main thing which spoils the image and attracts abuse by others, please be cautious with your cleaning up. Remember that what adults see as junk can often be essential den-building material to the local kids. So far as the wildlife is concerned, most of this junk, which looks so awful, is actually doing no harm at all. In fact for some species it is a positive benefit. I mentioned the clumps of nettles that are a sign of high fertility, around the spot where people dump their garden clippings. All that rotting vegetation is marvellous habitat for slugs, snails and a whole collection of creepy-crawlies that thrive on decay. They in

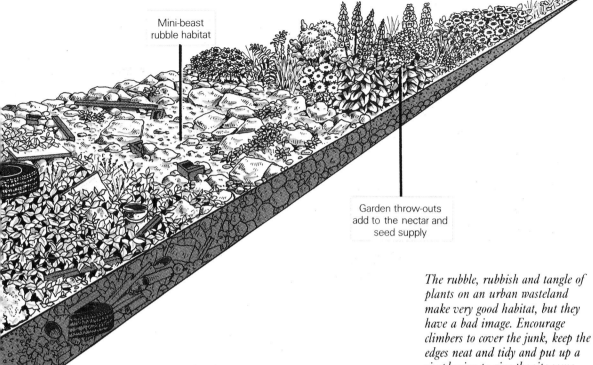

Mini-beast
rubble habitat

Garden throw-outs
add to the nectar and
seed supply

The rubble, rubbish and tangle of plants on an urban wasteland make very good habitat, but they have a bad image. Encourage climbers to cover the junk, keep the edges neat and tidy and put up a simple sign to give the site some identity.

turn bring in the birds, the hedgehogs and the shrews. The inorganic junk can be valuable, too. A pile of old bicycle frames and pots and pans may look unsightly, but it doesn't take long for wild creatures to find a way of using it. After all, where would nesting robins be without abandoned kettles? One very good way of improving your rubbish-tip site is to build new habitats with the junk itself. Some of the metal will be recyclable, of course, and you may be able to arrange for it to be carted away for the value of the scrap. You might even find it earns you a few bob to pay for other improvements. A great deal of the remaining material can be recycled on site. Divide the junk into five categories: metal and angular things like bike frames, TV aerials and plastic drainpipes; stone and rubble; timber; vegetable rubbish such as bags of lawn clippings and rose prunings; and sheets of plastic, paint pots and other 'non-biodegradable' or potentially toxic waste. The last category is the only one you really can't use. Chemicals are obviously hazardous, and plastic is just so persistent in the landscape that you had best get rid of it completely. Don't do what one eager group I know did, and cart your unwanted

plastic junk down the road to the next patch of wasteland.
Take it to the council tip.

The smelly, gungy, rotting vegetable matter should be
heaped in one or two spots where it can quietly get on with the
job of decomposing. If the garden refuse is likely to be a
recurring problem, then it may well be worth building a
proper compost bin, and putting a notice up inviting people
to tip their waste there. If you want to be really sophisticated,
have a bay for twiggy waste, which will take a long time to rot
down, and a couple of bays for the softer stuff, so that one
can be composting whilst the other is filling up. The actual
organisms of decomposition will quickly find the banquet,
and they, in turn, will attract predators. When the compost
has fully rotted down it can be returned to people's gardens
as fertiliser, or used to grow the biggest and best nettle patch
in the area. Certainly a big patch of unsprayed nettles will
dramatically boost the breeding success of several of the more
colourful species of butterflies. Remember that nettle leaves
are the essential food for the larvae of peacock, small
tortoiseshell and red admiral butterflies. If you want the best
possible results, cut some of the nettles down in late spring.
This encourages new soft green shoots to sprout in
mid-summer, and so provides ideal conditions for July and
August egg-laying.

The pile of scrap metal, angle iron, clothes racks, pram
frames and the like can be used as the support structure
for a wonderful wildlife habitat. Pile up the junk, well away
from public view if possible, and try to stack it so that it is
good and solid, but with lots of spaces inside the heap. It's
then simply a matter of encouraging scrambling and
climbing plants to engulf it. Brambles are the obvious first
choice, because they grow quickly and keep their colourful
leaves through much of the winter. Ivy is an excellent plant
too. It is completely evergreen, of course, and produces both
flowers and fruits which are of enormous value to wildlife.
Wild dog rose will scramble over your metal wigwam given
half a chance, and you may like to introduce something a little
more exotic. Wild hop, for instance, is an alternative food
plant to nettles for the caterpillars of comma butterflies. There
are garden plants worth considering too. *Clematis montana*, for
example, produces masses of pretty pink perfumed flowers in
May, and grows like mad. Russian vine is another vigorous
garden climber, or there are various varieties of honeysuckle,
all of which have richly perfumed flowers which will attract

moths in the evening. For the very quickest covering, some of the climbing annuals are difficult to beat. Climbing nasturtium will grow well on the poorest of soil, its colourful flowers are full of nectar and keep on coming right through the summer, and its leaves are a caterpillar food plant for cabbage white butterflies. Nasturtium is also a favourite with blackfly, and whilst you may not wish to encourage such unwelcome wildlife in your garden, out in the local wild patch they will provide a valuable source of food for the smaller insect-eating birds. If you let your canopy of tangled climbers weave and wind itself over the scrap-pile, then you will have the perfect hidy-hole for a fox's daytime lair, or for species such as wrens, robins, blackbirds and hedge dunnocks to nest in.

The stone and rubble can be used in several ways to improve your site. It may be useful simply to mark the route people should take through your newly renamed wildlife sanctuary. Simply line-up old bricks and kerbstones along both sides of your preferred path and it will help steer most people where you want them to go. That means you can reduce disturbance in the orchid patch or amongst the nesting birds.

The stones and rubble are also useful, simply as the basis of a 'mini-beast' area. By concentrating the stones in one area, preferably over fairly infertile soil, visiting children in particular can be guaranteed interesting animals to study whenever they care to visit. Once the rubble has settled down, all kinds of weird-looking creatures will take up residence in the dark damp beneath the stones. Woodlice will probably be the most common, but ground beetles, millipedes,

White bryony is one of the native climbers you can train over junk. Its tendrils will cling to anything. Bees love the flowers, and the strings of orange fruit are very colourful, but they are poisonous.

NATIVE WASTELAND WILDFLOWERS

Refugees from the cornfield, all of which thrive on disturbance.

Corncockle	*Agrostemma githago*
Scarlet pimpernel	
	Anagallis arvensis
Shepherd's purse	
	Capsella bursapastoris
Fat-hen	*Chenopodium album*
Corn marigold	
	Chrysanthemum segetum
Chicory	*Cichorium intybus*
Creeping thistle	*Cirsium arvense*
Red deadnettle	
	Lamium purpureum
Pineapple mayweed	
	Matricaria matricarioides
Common poppy	*Papaver rhoeas*
Annual meadow grass	*Poa annua*
Redshanks	*Polygonum persicaria*
Creeping buttercup	
	Ranunculus repens
Groundsel	*Senecio vulgaris*
Garlic mustard	*Sisymbrium officinale*
Smooth sowthistle	*Sonchus oleraceus*
Common chickweed	
	Stellaria media
Coltsfoot	*Tussilago farfara*
Stinging nettle	*Urtica dioica*
White deadnettle	*Lamium album*
Charlock	*Sinapis arvensis*
Teasel	*Dipsacus fullonum*
Couch grass	*Agropyron repens*
Scentless mayweed	
	Matricaria maritima
Tansy	*Tanacetum vulgare*
Marjoram	*Origanum vulgare*
Cornflower	*Centaurea cyanus*
Weld	*Reseda luteola*
Toadflax	*Linaria vulgaris*

centipedes, slugs, snails and worms will live there too, and in the winter months you may well have the excitement of discovering a hibernating newt or two. Although it is fun to study mini-beasts, it is very important to remember that they are real live animals, not toys. They must be handled very carefully, preferably by lifting them gently into a viewing box for safety. I use a super little device called a bug-box when I'm on safari for mini-beasts. This is a small, clear plastic cube, with a lens in the lid, available in toy shops, and cheap enough for you to have plenty available. A shortage of boxes can be disastrous, as it leads to enthusiastic collectors mixing their finds and then making the earth-shattering discovery that some kinds of mini-beasts eat others. Once the mini-beasts have been carefully studied, then it should go without saying that they must always be returned carefully to their homes, and the stone lowered gently back into place.

If you have lots of stone waste, then you may not want to cover huge areas with mini-beast habitat. If this is the case, then why not build a dry stone wall habitat? This can be a marvellous place to grow wildflowers such as herb robert, stonecrop and harebell: species which thrive in really well drained spots.

It will also provide a concentration of nooks, crannies and crevices in a relatively small area, and will quickly attract such creatures as wrens, robins, weasels and toads. We included one of these habitats in the landscape around the new Victoria Theatre in Stoke-on-Trent, and within a week, a family of wood mice had moved in. The construction is quite simple, though the work can be rather heavy, so little children will need a lot of help. Always begin with the biggest stones at the bottom, and aim to build two walls, back to back. Leave plenty of space in the gap between, to be filled up with loose rubble and sub-soil. If you have plenty of space you might like to build a circle, or a biggish square, and then you could fill it with the bigger junk such as old washing machines as well as the rubble. Make the walls as solid as you can, by packing the big stones with small bits and pieces, or with soil, and do try to leave plenty of little holes through into the spaces within. You can top off your rubble-wall habitat with flat slabs if there are any, or you might like to plant it up with shrubs and turn it into a kind of urban hedge bank. Buddleia bushes grow really well in this kind of rubbly spot.

If you have only a small number of stones left over after the mini-beast area is complete, try building them to seat-height and topping them off with an old railway sleeper. A seat in a nice sheltered spot is the best way to make people sit and watch quietly, and you will be boosting the habitat, too.

Talking of seats reminds me that there is bags of scope for using your imagination with wasteland junk. On a site near home I worked for a whole Sunday with lots of local people, clearing up the various kinds of dumped rubbish. For some reason there were an awful lot of old car tyres amongst the junk, and two enterprising lads made some luxurious benches by building piles of tyres in pairs, and then fixing a plank across the top. As you sat on the plank, the tyres wheezed and hissed a little, and settled an inch or two, to give you the most comfortable, springy seat imaginable.

With the compost, the scrap metal and the rubble all used up, and the plastic and poisons carted away to a proper tip, the only thing left should be the timber. I think most people know that dead logs and old tree trunks are a very important part of woodland habitat, providing a home for a whole range of interesting wood-boring beetles, toadstools and the like. The timber you find dumped on your gap-site is likely to be window-frame and door shaped, and covered in paint – but don't let that put you off. Beneath every chunk of gloss-painted window-frame there lurks a dead branch just dying to become wildlife habitat. Saw, chop or break up your timber into less recognisable lumps, pile them on an area of soil where the organisms of decay can get at them, and your 'log pile' will quickly develop a wildlife community all of its own.

All of this heaving around of junk can be great fun, and you're likely to recruit an awful lot of helpers very quickly. On that little site in Brixton we began throwing our unusable junk into a skip at ten o'clock on a Sunday morning, and by eleven o'clock, over twenty helpers had joined in. Most of them were under the age of twelve, and that does create a problem, because some of the junk can be quite dangerous with sharp points and fragments of broken glass. You need to take your responsibility for children seriously. One very simple thing I always do is have a wad of sticky labels, preferably with a picture of some sort on the front. As the new recruits arrive they are labelled clearly with their name and address. They are then asked to run home and tell parents where they are. This procedure helps in lots of ways. Firstly, word gets round and a stream of extra kids turn up 'to join'. Secondly, everyone can see the badges, and is immediately on first name terms. That helps break the ice. Thirdly,

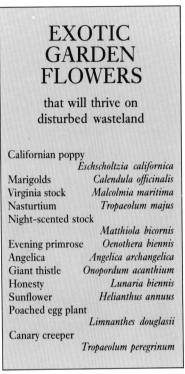

EXOTIC GARDEN FLOWERS

that will thrive on disturbed wasteland

Californian poppy	
	Eschscholtzia californica
Marigolds	*Calendula officinalis*
Virginia stock	*Malcolmia maritima*
Nasturtium	*Tropaeolum majus*
Night-scented stock	
	Matthiola bicornis
Evening primrose	*Oenothera biennis*
Angelica	*Angelica archangelica*
Giant thistle	*Onopordum acanthium*
Honesty	*Lunaria biennis*
Sunflower	*Helianthus annuus*
Poached egg plant	
	Limnanthes douglasii
Canary creeper	
	Tropaeolum peregrinum

All this energy is a marvellous resource if it finds a positive outlet. These particular friends of mine created a nature garden out of a patch of tipped wasteland on their housing estate in Brixton.

supervision is made much more effective if the chilling name 'Jason' or 'Tracy' can be hurled accurately across the site when things begin to get out of hand, and, of course, if there is an accident, the injured volunteer can be whisked quickly home. In all the days of volunteer parties I have helped to run, I've only ever had one serious accident, but the way it happened may help you to avoid a similar upset. We had been clearing junk on a cold winter's day, and to keep warm and increase the general fun we'd burned a good deal of the less useful rubbish on a bonfire. Over seventy people had turned up, the work had all been done, and most people had drifted home by about four o'clock. There was just a small group of nine and ten-year-old lads, chatting knowledgeably around the dying embers, for all the world like village elders.

Suddenly there was a single piercing scream, and a silence
from the rest of the group which you could have cut with a
knife. One of the little treasures had picked up a three foot
long piece of rusty metal, and swung it casually round his
head. Unfortunately, it connected with the mouth of the lad
next to him, knocking out a front tooth, and slicing through
his lip. Luckily, I had a car, and was able to bundle him off
to the hospital whilst someone else contacted his mum and
dad. An hour later I was back on site, grovelling on hands
and knees in search of the missing tooth, which amazingly
enough we did find, and apparently the doctor managed a
successful replant. Accidents like that can happen so easily.
It's a split-second affair, and it always happens when you've
relaxed, and your attention has lapsed a little. To be absolutely
professional, I strongly advise that all volunteers are asked
to get a tetanus injection – it is surprising how few adults have
them, though with young children it is now a matter of course.
Rusty nails, piles of rubbish and soil can be a very dodgy
combination. I also suggest that you try to take out a personal
accident insurance policy if you can. The British Trust for
Conservation Volunteers is a charitable trust which is
particularly geared up to working with volunteers on practical
projects. They have a cheap and simple policy available to
affiliated organisations, but, unfortunately, even this specific
policy doesn't cover anyone under twelve years of age.

The only way children can be insured easily is by the blanket
cover which will apply if they get involved as a member of
a school party. Youth groups such as WATCH, Young
Ornithologists, cubs or brownies tend to have insurance
policies which protect the leaders against claims from the
children in their care.

One other word of caution is very important when it comes
to shifting junk around, or carrying out any kind of major
habitat disturbance. Do make sure you put the well-being of
wildlife first at all times, and choose a good time of year.
The golden rule is to avoid any kind of disruptive work during
the breeding season. That means from mid-March, when
the first of the blackbirds will be nesting and the frogs will be
spawning, right through until August, by which time the last of
the spotted flycatchers will have fledged. Any disturbance
during that six-month period will be damaging. There is no
point relocating a rusty kettle from the fly-tipping pile to the
new super scrap habitat, if the robins have already nested
and laid their eggs in the thing before you start. For the past

*The Tulse Hill Nature Garden –
created from wasteland, by local
kids, for everyone to enjoy.*

few years, 'Keep Britain Tidy' and the scout and guide movement have combined forces for a massive environmental clean-up week. That's a fine idea in principle, but year after year they have chosen a week in April, right in the middle of the nesting season, and I dread to think how much damaging disturbance has resulted.

Finally, there are one or two things you might do to improve the rubble habitat by planting. The temptation is always to plant trees. They are big, and obvious, and you can get a grant for them. Do beware, though. There is little point planting a tree on a site with an uncertain future, and in any case, this kind of habitat may be more useful for other kinds of vegetation. The plants I would choose to introduce to urban wasteland are the typical garden throw-outs. Every gardener has clumps of certain plants which are invasive, and start to become a nuisance. These make marvellous wasteland introductions, and they need very little encouragement once they arrive. Try advertising an amnesty for garden throw-outs, around October. Stick a few postcards up in local shops, have an announcement made at a meeting of a local gardening club, and stand by to receive boarders. The kinds of plants you can expect will mostly be herbaceous perennials, and whilst few of them will have leaves of much value to wildlife, they will tend to have bright flowers, a mass of nectar and pollen and, probably, a good crop of seed to follow. Favourites you can expect include Michaelmas daisy, golden rod, red hot poker, horseradish, London pride, leopards bane, rudbeckia, gardeners' garters, lupins, cranesbill, snow in summer and montbretia. Old raspberry canes are very useful, and so are shrubs such as snowberry, Oregon grape and sumac. If the plants come with any soil at all, just dump them 'green-side-up' on open ground, and give them a good soaking if you can. Then all you need to do is stand back and watch them grow.

The biggest threat to this kind of disturbed site, apart from the obvious one of development, is that of 'establishment'. It is at its most interesting when it is recently disturbed, and full of vigorously competing wild plants and animals. After a year or two it is likely to settle down. The most aggressive plants push out everything else, and the site loses much of its interest. If you really want to keep your urban rubble site looking at its weediest and most colourful, then the best thing you can possibly do is give it a good going over every year or two.

NEW LIFE IN OLD PARKS

8

So far I've talked about our public parks and open spaces rather rudely as 'green deserts', but that is not really fair. There was a time when they were the envy of the world. Before the industrial revolution no one needed such things. The rich had their own private estates, and the poor lived mainly in the fresh air of the countryside. Once the industrial cities began to grow, things changed very quickly. The new 'aristocracy' of mill-owners and other 'bosses' were forced to live in the grimy towns, and of course the workers had little or no chance of escaping to the countryside either.

The idea of a city park began in the town of Birkenhead, of all places, just across the Mersey from the boom city of Liverpool. Joseph Paxton came up with the idea. This was the same man who designed Crystal Palace and was head gardener to the Duke of Devonshire at Chatsworth. Birkenhead Park was intended first and foremost to be a clever money-making venture. Paxton and his cronies knew that the richer managerial and professional classes would happily pay a premium for houses which overlooked a patch of green inner-city 'countryside'. Avenues were planted. Grassy mounds were built, lakes were dug, and a formalised countryside was created in the city. As a bonus to this real-estate motive the park provided a place for fresh air and recreation for the exploited and otherwise 'town-locked' workers. If you look carefully at any of our older city parks you will notice that they have extremely wide paths. This is because they were originally designed to allow two ladies in crinolines to pass one another! A stroll in the park was an important form of social recreation, and I have no doubt that in their heyday our city parks were very popular and very busy. The problem is that times have changed a great deal, and many parks have failed to keep up.

Interestingly enough, whilst city parks in Britain developed

as a kind of poor man's stately home, with formal avenues of exotic trees, rolling lawns and intricate patterns of carpet bedding, the basic idea was adapted very differently abroad. An American landscape architect, Frederick Law Ormstead, came over to England, saw Birkenhead Park, and then went on to visit prettier parts of rural England. When he went back home, he used this tour as the inspiration for Central Park, New York. Again there was the idea of high-value speculative building around a green city space, but instead of the rigid formality of Victorian Britain, Ormstead created a patch of rolling 'English' countryside, with streams and lakes, woodlands and meadows. This, he felt, was what the crowded city-dwellers of New York longed for. Now, over a century later, we are beginning to realise that 'captive countryside' is something people in Britain long for, too, and our rich legacy of Victorian public parks is a land of golden opportunity. No one seems to know just how much land is involved, but I would guess we have at least a quarter of a million acres. The City of Birmingham alone has 1700 acres, and towns and cities like Sheffield, Rotherham, Manchester and Glasgow, with a particularly 'dirty' industrial history, are often the places with the biggest acreage of public open space. Most of the possibilities which parks can offer apply equally well to other municipally maintained landscapes. There are over 100,000 acres of green desert around our schools, for example, not to mention hospitals, universities and colleges. With so little land available for wildlife in the countryside these days, and with no requirement for all this official parkland to be productive, it seems immoral to me to spend so much public money thoughtlessly suppressing nature. These hallowed green acres are the rich, accessible countryside of the future, and as taxpayers and ratepayers it is up to all of us to bring about that change, by telling councillors and park keepers that we want more butterflies and skylarks, and fewer sterile deserts.

Public parks really do have a great deal going for them. They are publicly owned, and most of them are secured in trust for ever as public open spaces – so we really can think long term. Nobody is going to take them away. Even in these hard times they do have a substantial labour force. Many parks workers have been demoralised and de-skilled over the past decade or two, and their levels of pay are scandalously low. There are, however, a surprising number of people working in parks who wouldn't want to do anything else and who take

Why can't more parks look like this? Dense multi-canopied woodland belts provide shelter for people, and marvellous habitat for wildlife.

great pride in their job: they are eager to see changes, and
to begin building up a closer relationship with local people
once again. Many of them are passionate about nature, and
long to have more wildflowers, birds and butterflies around
them. The reason they give for hanging back is the number of
complaints they get from the tidy-minded 'telephone and lace
curtain' brigade, who wield such power with local
councillors. The will is there to bring more wildlife into parks.
It makes economic sense. It would make much more positive
use of the land involved and it would capture the imagination
of many more people, and of children in particular. The
only thing stopping it is the tiny pile of letters that hit the
parks director's desk the month the daisies 'get out of
control'. It is a ridiculously small number of 'Victorians' who
stifle parks' initiatives. If you really want to see a change for
the better, then it is ordinary people who hold the key. Write
even more letters to the director, making an even bigger pile
on his desk, but this time in praise of daisies, dandelions,
cowslips, dragonflies, songbirds and all the other things you
want to see and hear in your local park. In many cases that is
all the director and the parks staff are waiting for.

I imagine by now that you are beginning to think this is all
a bit fanciful. How can one little individual like you change
a whole huge landscape? Well, in a way, the 'tidy-minded
moaners' have already proved that it is possible. By issuing
a relentless stream of complaints, they have kept grass shaved,
dead branches and autumn leaves swept away, and boating
lakes completely free of 'messy' vegetation. They have

Single
trees

Close-mown
grass

manipulated the spending of thousands of millions of pounds each year, and kept our municipal landscapes bland, boring, and unloved by both people and wildlife. You have a much more positive contribution to make, and you know *why* you want your park to be wilder, to have more seasonal change, and to be more stimulating to the senses.

Direct your first letters to the chairman of the parks committee. He or she is a councillor, not a paid officer, and will be pleased to hear from someone 'on the ground'. Ask for a meeting in the park, where you can explain the kind of things you would prefer to see, and make it clear that you are willing to help. You won't be expected to turn up with a mowing machine, but you could offer to help explain the changes to local people, or organise a meeting for the neighbours, where the parks staff can exchange ideas.

In many towns, local people are beginning to form groups specifically to influence their park. Why not suggest a 'Friends of . . .' group? It doesn't need to be an elaborate affair, but you will find that the parks department will be very happy to meet, perhaps twice a year, for a walk through the park and an exchange of ideas. The city of Bristol now has 'Friends' groups for most of its parks, and partly as a result of these, there is now much more wildlife habitat appearing there. Local schools are becoming more involved, too. In Birmingham we have a marvellous project underway, where hundreds of local children, helped by teachers, parents and the Urban Wildlife Group, are preparing their own proposals for the improvement of an open space which really is a green desert at the moment. The children are asking for 'jungle' and squidgy muddy areas, places to build dens and fish for tadpoles, and the parks department have already

Municipal parks and open spaces tend to be a sterile combination of close-mown grass, a few tired old trees and, if you're lucky, a lifeless, concrete-edged boating lake . . .

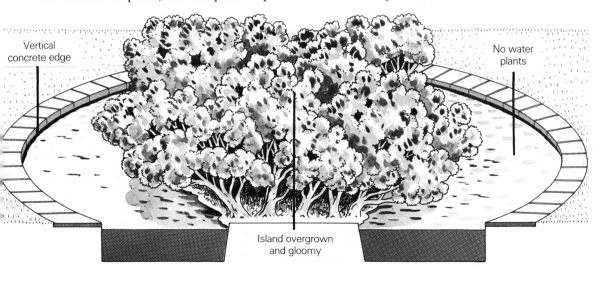

Vertical concrete edge

No water plants

Island overgrown and gloomy

Most parks, however well cared for, tend to be sterile and lifeless.

Carpet-bedding is an important part of our heritage. I would hate to lose it, but there must be room for natural landscapes too.

put in a big pond as a move towards a wilder landscape. The revolution can start with you.

All but the poshest of parks have little more than close-mown grass, trees and play equipment in them. There is sometimes a tired shrubbery or two, to hide the public lavatories, and if you are lucky there may be a concrete-lined pond or lake – long since relieved of its rowing boats. If there is still any of that colourful carpet bedding left, it will probably be confined to a couple of diamond-shaped beds by the main gate. The scope for improvement here is tremendous.

Try making the point that, by relaxing and restructuring the management of more remote corners of the park, there would be greater scope for the wildlife, more of a countryside atmosphere, and perhaps a chance to concentrate more of the dwindling resources into intensive elements such as carpet bedding. Some of the border plants which parks use are a valuable wildlife resource anyway. As a general rule, tightly packed double flowers are less valuable than simple single blooms. In fact quite a few of the modern exotic hybrids are completely sterile and offer neither nectar nor pollen to the bumblebees and butterflies. Suggest that you would like to see more pollen and nectar plants, and that a simple interpretation board, with pictures of the more common insects, would help people gain even more enjoyment from the flowers in the park. Encourage the parks department to experiment. Suggest they plant one border with 'goodies'

such as tobacco plant (*Nicotiana affinis*), cherry pie
(*Heliotropium × hybridum*), white alyssum, single petunias,
ageratum and another with 'barren' flowers such as double
pelargoniums (geraniums), double petunias and exotic
foliage bedding like coleus. Ask a local junior school to monitor
the two beds for insect life, and from then on you'll have
the basis for a very fruitful co-operation.

One feature in many of the older parks and public open
spaces is a population of native, often majestic trees. In some
cases these are all that remain of an ancient woodland which
occupied the site before the industrial revolution. In other
cases there are exotic parkland trees – cedars of Lebanon,
tulip trees and horse chestnuts for example, planted as part
of an ornamental scheme when the park was first laid out.

The native trees are of much greater value to wildlife than
the foreign exotics, since again they provide vital food for
native animal life. An English oak, for example, has over 240
different species of insects which depend upon it, whilst an
exotic and colourful North American red oak supports fewer
than ten. Whatever the species may be, though, these big
parkland trees have one valuable characteristic, and that is
their size. Nothing we plant now is going to reach their
stature for many years, and in the case of big forest trees such
as oak, beech and lime, you are looking at an investment of
at least a century and a half, before you have a hope of
achieving anything of similar size and value.

*There are old forest trees in many
of our parks, but they are lost in
a sea of mown grass.*

Some of these trees are important simply as specimens – a
part of the parkland heritage in their own right – and the
common policy of planting occasional replacement individuals
is absolutely appropriate. Where there is an open group of
such native specimens, however, we have a wonderful
opportunity to recreate a genuine, diverse woodland habitat
in the space of just a few years. Find a group of mature
specimens which is not too close to a busy footpath if you
can, and expect to change it gradually, over a number of years.
Your objective should be to help a range of vegetation
canopies to redevelop, with tree seedlings growing through to
replenish the native tree cover, and a mixture of woodland
wildflowers and scrambling plants providing the ground
floor. There should be plenty of decay going on, since far
more species feed on dead plant material than on the living
stuff, and there should be undisturbed sanctuary areas set
aside to encourage the more timid species.

The first big breakthrough comes when you manage to

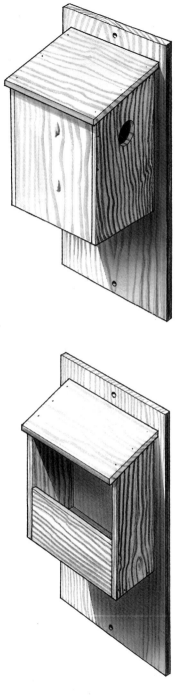

persuade the councillors, in particular, that a landscape can be made more enjoyable, rather than less, if you are unable to walk about on every square inch of it. There is an unwritten rule in many parks departments that every corner of a park must be easily accessible, and that is what leads us to spend so much money mowing grass beneath the 'woodland' canopy. If there is resistance to the idea, arrange a walk for the councillors through a real wood, and a patch of farmland, and point out how much more interesting the narrow footpath is, precisely because there are inaccessible 'sanctuary areas' on either side.

There may not be a need actually to fence off areas of your proposed park-woodland. A well-signed, close-mown or bark-surfaced path through the area will effectively encourage most people to keep out of the remaining zones. If there is a serious problem with 'trespass and trampling', then a temporary fence, erected for a couple of seasons, will generally give the habitat a chance to get going, and after that the fence can be taken down and used elsewhere.

Reduced trampling is vital, if stage one of the rehabilitation programme is to happen. When you first start you will probably have the vicious circle of universal public access creating the need for regular mowing and leaf sweeping, and a clinical policy of tree-surgery to remove any branch which has the remotest chance of dropping off and hitting a member of the public. To give woodland wildlife the slightest hope of re-establishing, the first move must be to stop mowing the grass, to allow the leaf-litter to lie where it falls, and to tolerate dead branches and decay within the trees. Obviously this more relaxed policy needs to be tempered with caution. Trees which are very close to paths should continue to be pruned – particularly if the dying branches in question overhang the public – but when these branches do need to be cut off, they should be left to rot on the woodland floor, where they will still support the dependent invertebrate life, the fungi and so on. Left on the tree, these branches would provide nesting sites for such hole-nesting birds as bluetits and great tits, starlings, woodpeckers and tawny owls.

As part of the first phase of rehab, it is well worth placing a number of nest-boxes in the trees, to compensate for the lack of holes. Again this is a marvellous project for local children to join in with. If the nest-boxes are made at home, or perhaps at school, and then presented to the parks department for them to put in place, they will melt the heart

of the stoniest director. Number the boxes, and the young
volunteers can then keep a careful watch on their new
high-rise nesting estate, and begin to keep records which will
help to improve the scheme in future years. Which hole size
is best for bluetits? Which height of nest-box do various birds
seem to prefer? How many journeys do the parents make in
an hour to find food for the chicks?

Once the mowing stops, you will find all kinds of plants
appear, which were never given a chance before. If you are
very lucky you may even find a tiny relic of the woodland
wildflower community, with such species as violets, bluebells
and celandines popping up and flowering. The only plant you
really don't want to see is sycamore. If you have mature
sycamore in your 'woodland', then grass cutting will have
chopped off the thousands of seedlings each spring, and
stopped them taking over. Remove the mower, and you can
have a forest of sycamore seedlings in no time. You may feel
this can only be a good thing – they are trees, after all.
Sycamores aren't all bad. They do produce juicy leaves and
support millions of greenfly, and bluetits, in particular, make
good use of these sticky little sap-suckers as food for fledglings
in early spring. Generally though, sycamore is pretty bad news
for wildlife. It grows very vigorously and its broad leaves
shade out all other species very quickly. It is not native to
Britain, and consequently very few types of invertebrates
feed on its leaves. When autumn arrives, the leaves form a
suffocating layer which kills off most of the few wildflowers
which may have survived the dense summer shade, and of
course it does keep churning out an amazing number of very
successful helicopters, year after year. If sycamores form only
a small proportion of the trees in your group, then it is worth
seriously considering killing them. This is easy to do, by
stripping the bark in a belt all the way around the trunk,
though you are likely to get a super-crop of seed in a last,
dying effort for survival, and you will certainly get a
tremendous cluster of suckers around the base which will
need to be coppiced back every couple of years. Leave the
dead tree standing, perhaps removing some of the bigger
branches if they could be dangerous. Leaving the tree
upright in this way lessens the risk of wind blow for the
adjacent trees, and can have a spectacular impact on the
woodpecker population, providing drumming, feeding and
nesting facilities all in one go.

Sycamore seedlings are best left until they are two or three

OPPOSITE: *Many different species
of birds will nest in boxes. Robins,
blackbirds and spotted flycatchers
use the ones with an open front;
bluetits, great tits and starlings
prefer the small hole. The species
you attract will depend on the size
of the hole: 1 inch diameter for
bluetits; 1¼ inch for great tits; 1½
inch for tree sparrows and 1¾ inch
for starlings. A box with a floor 6
inches square will cater for most
birds.*

years old, and then pulled out by hand – roots and all. Bigger plants can be cut hard back to encourage leafy suckers, and provided this is repeated every three years or so, you will have the benefit of aphids for the bluetits without either the overwhelming shade or the problem of further seed colonisation. Sycamore-bashing is one very practical way in which you and your friends can help the local park department, once they start trying to encourage new woodland habitat.

The other woody plant which frequently crops up immediately you stop mowing is bramble. Generally speaking this is a good plant to encourage, since it is a native, supporting lots of leaf-eating species. Its flowers are a popular source of nectar and pollen, especially for gatekeeper and comma butterflies; blackberries are a favourite autumn food for birds and small mammals, and its prickly stems create safe nesting sites, and a useful barrier to human disturbance.

The developing tangle of undergrowth does look more untidy than the mown grass, but it costs much less to manage, and provided the approved paths are given a well maintained border, just as I suggested with wasteland, then people will quickly accept the change. Within as little as two years, this simple reduction in the intensity of maintenance will produce a noticeable increase in the numbers of songbirds and insects. Provide a small notice or two, simply telling people what is happening, and what to look for, and very quickly you will find that there is a loyal band of watchers, eager to make more nest-boxes, help with litter collection, or join in with the next stage of habitat development.

A long-established wood will contain a rich variety of native shrubs, all able to cope with the shade from the trees above. Your new park woodland will have very few of those shrub species present, and so the next task is to plant some. The best way of deciding what to plant is to go and look at the nearest 'natural' wood growing on similar soil in your area, and to see what grows there. Your local County Wildlife Trust will be able to help, or the local council itself may have a forestry officer or even a local authority ecologist.

Typical shrub species of deciduous lowland woodlands are hazel, holly, wild privet, hawthorn, dogrose and buckthorn, and all of these are available from tree and shrub nurseries. You should be able to persuade the parks department to provide the plants themselves, of course, since all of them spend thousands of pounds every year buying and planting trees and shrubs, but do make sure they only provide native

species. They have a strong tendency to slip in the odd rhododendron or azalea, and however pretty these may be, they are a nightmare in woodland which is intended for encouraging wildlife.

The ideal way of obtaining plants for your new wood is by collecting either seeds or cuttings from plants already growing in the neighbourhood, and propagating them in your own nursery.

The shrubs should be planted during the dormant season, from leaf-fall through to the end of April; I suggest you space them about a yard and a half apart, and in groups of ten or more of a single species. Leave some areas unplanted too, to allow more light through to the wildflower layer. It is quite a good idea to plant prickly species such as hawthorn, dogrose and holly along the edge of the wood, and if you pack

This pretty woodland path is in the Jac. P. Thijse park in Amstelveen, near Amsterdam, Holland. It contains only native woodland wildflowers, but the sheets of wood anemone, primrose, lily of the valley, violet and celandine are cared for just like any other detailed planting scheme, and the result is exquisite.

them a little closer together they will quickly intertwine and help to protect the sanctuary areas from disturbance.

The shrub layer is very important for wildlife, since it provides food and shelter for a very wide range of species. There is a need to promote replacement tree seedlings to renew the high canopy too, and in many situations you can expect seedlings to arrive spontaneously. Once the leaf-litter begins to build up, jays will start to carry in acorns to hide. Inevitably some of them will be forgotten, and will pop up as seedlings. In fact, this really is the best way to establish oak, and if the jays don't oblige then a morning of local harvesting followed by an afternoon of acorn planting is great fun, and something you can quietly get on with all on your own if need be. Hazel can be introduced in just the same way, but smaller seeds than these really do need the help of a nursery bed or a plant pot to start them off.

One of the habitat boosters that is often available in parks is leaf-litter. Thousands of tons of leaves are swept from streets, footpaths, sports pitches and car parks every autumn, and very few councils bother to do anything positive with them. As often as not they are simply burned. Our new

Boundary hedge   New woodland understorey   Meadow-length grass

woodland habitat will benefit enormously if some of those leaves can be brought in and spread over the ground in the early years. They will help keep the root zone moist for newly planted shrubs, and they will also provide food for the organisms of decay which in turn provide a livelihood for foraging blackbirds and hedgehogs.

Some of those leaves should be packed into black polythene bags, and stacked in a quiet corner somewhere, until they turn into soft, dark, crumbly leaf-mould. This makes a valuable additive to seed compost for the next job, which is growing wildflowers for the woodland.

Again it is best to collect wild seed from your own area, though you must ask permission if the wildflowers are rare. Such species as foxglove, hedge woundwort, garlic mustard and red campion are still common enough, and a few ripe seeds shaken into your paper bag, rather than back on to the ground, will have little or no damaging effect. Less common species such as primrose, wood anemone and yellow archangel are quite a different story, and you may have to resort to buying nursery-grown seed from one of the reliable seed suppliers, though more and more County Trusts are beginning to collect and sell seed from their nature reserves. Local seed is always best, so do check with your own local Trust, to see if they can help.

Again there are important resources available within the parks departments themselves. Although large scale bedding plant production is a thing of the past, and some councils have resorted to buying all their plants from private nurseries,

. . . By varying the mowing regime to produce meadows, planting hedges around the boundaries, underplanting old trees with a shrub and wildflower layer and creating shallow edges to the lake, a sterile park can quickly be made into a rich bit of 'countryside'.

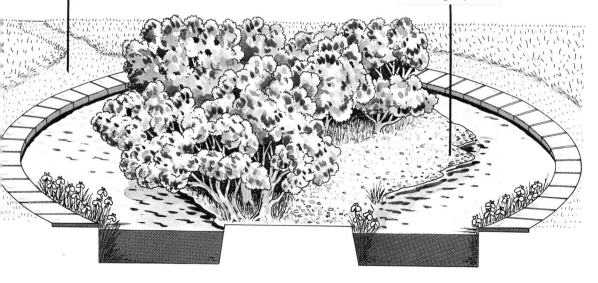

Mown grass paths

Island part cleared and margins planted

the vast majority do still have a plant production unit. The skill you need to grow a good tray of polyanthus for the traffic island can just as easily be employed in growing primroses. You only need to ask. This is something that green-fingered individuals can do too. A great many people who aren't too keen on the heavier work of tree planting or log stacking, will jump at the chance of helping in a more genteel way by growing plants. I wanted sheets of primroses, cowslips, violets, campion and foxgloves to complete the landscape around the new Victoria Theatre near Stoke-on-Trent. These could have been purchased, pot-grown, from one of the specialist wildflower nurseries. Instead we arranged for keen volunteers to receive packets of seed and compost, and six months later seed-trays, plant pots and margarine tubs full of beautifully healthy wildflower seedlings began to arrive on site, and every one was accompanied by a proud volunteer with a beaming smile.

The wildflowers do best where there is a reasonable amount of dappled shade filtering through. If your old trees are rather thin, then you may be able to plant throughout the wood, but with limited resources it is generally best to concentrate this colour along the edges of paths and around the perimeter of the wood. Again you should plant the seedlings in groups, at spacings of about twelve to eighteen inches, and of course once the wildflowers settle in they will provide you with a very convenient supply of fresh seed each

This is a Dutch wildflower meadow. It is very wet, and full of marsh marigolds in spring, ragged robin and meadow buttercups in summer. For thirty years the parks department has managed it to encourage wildlife.

year, and further plant production will be simplified.

I will talk about the actual long-term management of woodland in chapter ten, but there is one further boost that you can give your newly emerging woodland. Whilst wildflowers are available as packets of seeds, and birds, mammals and many of the insects are mobile enough to seek out and colonise the habitat themselves, there is a wealth of 'secret' wildlife living on the woodland floor, which will never reach your wood unless it gets a helping hand. Once you have established the beginnings of a genuine habitat, the shrubs are growing and the grass is being replaced by woodland wildflowers, make another approach to the manager of one of your better local woods. The local County Wildlife Trust will probably be able to help with a name. Choose a site with similar soils and tree species to yours, and ask permission to transfer some of their leaf-litter and fallen timber to your park. If there are wet and dry patches in both sites, bring material from each area, and simply spread it around in appropriate parts of your new 'woodland'. You may find a range of wildflower seed is transferred in this way, but much more important, you will be re-introducing a source of woodland mini-beasts, and if your new habitat is working properly, they will quickly settle into their new location, and add even more to the woodland quality of your wild corner of the local park.

As a first step towards establishing wildflower meadows in parks and other public open spaces, it is worth taking a little trouble over choosing the best areas to begin. Intensively used sports pitches need to withstand heavy wear and tear, and they also need to be well drained if they are to cope with full use. They need to be reasonably flat too. It makes sense, therefore, to keep the deep, rich, well-drained, level sites for formal sports. That leaves us with a great many acres of grassland which could be better used as wildlife habitat. The steep slopes should perhaps be abandoned as grassland altogether, since they are so difficult to mow. Simple abandonment, with perhaps a little pump priming, would rapidly produce the early stages of shrub woodland, with broom and gorse, hawthorn and wild rose colonising the uncut grassland and producing an interesting new songbird habitat.

Where the grassland is the wrong shape for sports pitches, slopes a little too much or is just too small, or where there is a corner left over after pitches have been laid out, then there

SPRING MEADOW WILDFLOWERS

Plant into grassland left unmown from March to July. Cut and rake off in mid July, and keep short for the rest of the year.

Daisy	*Bellis perennis*
Catsear	*Hypochoeris radicata*
Cowslip	*Primula veris*
Bugle	*Ajuga reptans*
Selfheal	*Prunella vulgaris*
Speedwell	*Veronica chamaedrys*
Lesser stitchwort	*Stellaria graminea*
Fritillary	*Fritillaria meleagris*
Meadow saxifrage	
	Saxifraga granulata
Yellow rattle	*Rhinanthus minor*
Lady's smock *or* cuckoo flower	
	Cardamine pratensis

really should be no difficulty in persuading the parks department to adopt a wildflower meadow policy. The very best place to start is where the soil is poor, the grass is thin, and there is already a mosaic of 'lawn weeds' to be found. In the older parks and in landscapes such as those of Victorian schools and hospitals, there may have been a policy of continual cutting, with very little fertiliser added for a century or more, and in these circumstances certain wildflowers really thrive. Find a patch like this, and you can produce impressive results within a month. The 'weeds' in question are either low-growing creeping species such as cinquefoil, birdsfoot trefoil, speedwell, selfheal and lesser stitchwort, or they are rosette plants such as plantain, dandelion, daisy and catsear. In both cases, the plants can manage to survive for year after year, even if they are given no chance at all of flowering. If the blades of the parks mower are raised about one and a half inches, then the creeping species will produce sheets of pretty little flowers, and if mowing stops altogether for a month or so in the early summer, then the rosette plants will all send up flower stems and bloom. Do this on rich soils, and the grasses will leap a foot into the air, too, but on poor, infertile ground you will have the flowers and little else. I did this in the grounds of an old Victorian psychiatric hospital once, and produced a colourful flowery meadow within a month.

To make the most of this dormant meadow, there are three rules you must obey. Firstly, no chemicals! It should be obvious that herbicides and pesticides don't improve wildlife habitat, but in this case fertilisers are very damaging too, since they boost the grass growth and help to smother out the wildflowers. Secondly, this kind of meadow must be mown regularly throughout the growing season, except for the six-week break in late spring and early summer when the flowers are allowed to bloom. These weeds only survive in the grassland because the grass is short, and sunlight can get to their leaves. If you leave the meadow permanently uncut, then you may get plenty of wildflowers the first year, but by the second year most of the plants will have been killed by overshadowing.

The third rule is always to remove the clippings. If you fail to do this, then a thatch of dead grass quickly forms which prevents wildflowers from germinating or growing properly, and again boosts fertility making the suppressing grass grow stronger.

Real hay meadows stay uncut for three or four months of the growing season. No matter how weedy the lawns in the park already are, you will be lucky to find more than one or two true meadow wildflowers growing there. To survive in a meadow habitat the wildflowers' leaves have to be capable of competing for light with the taller grasses. Spring meadow flowers such as cowslip, lady's smock and bugle tend to do this by getting their whole flowering and seeding cycle over before the grasses reach full height, and spring meadows are particularly suitable for public parks, because if the hay is cut in June, the flowers will already have bloomed and seeded themselves, and the grass can be kept short enough through the rest of the summer to allow for fairly intensive formal use. Kickabout areas, picnic sites and summer camp sites could all be managed this way.

Summer meadows are cut much later in the season, and the wildflowers that grow there tend mainly to have flower stems with leaves all the way up them so that as the grass grows taller the flower stems simply keep up, and continue trapping energy-giving sunlight. Typical species of a tall summer meadow might include meadow buttercup, field scabious, salad burnet, ox-eye daisy and knapweed. If need be, this kind of community can be mown and raked off two or three times in early spring, to catch the end of the soccer season, and then in May or early June mowing should stop, and the grasses and wildflowers should be given their head. These taller, summer meadows can be extremely colourful, but they really are no-go areas for the public, since trampling damages them badly. This makes the maintenance of close-cut access paths through the taller grassland absolutely essential, and it is probably kind to stick up a warning notice for hay fever sufferers too.

In the case of both spring and summer meadows, there is a need for a tidying up cut in late September, and if you make this mowing really short, then the frosts of winter tend to set the grasses back a little, and the spring flowers seem to benefit.

Once a policy of meadow management has been agreed, there will be a need to introduce a greater range of appropriate wildflowers, since most of the weeds already there will not cope with the new regime forever. Although meadow wildflower seed is now readily available from several specialist seed nurseries, just simply scattering the seed over the grass with fingers crossed is almost a complete waste of time and money. The wildflowers must be established down in the soil, and that means using one of three techniques.

The most effective by far is to plant small pot-grown

SUMMER MEADOW WILDFLOWERS

Taller growing and able to compete with more vigorous grasses. Mow meadow frequently from spring until June, then allow sward to grow, and cut for hay in mid-September, when wildflower seed has ripened.

Greater knapweed	
	Centaurea scabiosa
Hardheads	*Centaurea nigra*
Meadow cranesbill	
	Geranium pratense
Field scabious	*Knautia arvensis*
Ox-eye daisy	*Leucanthemum vulgare*
Meadow buttercup	*Ranunculus acris*
Sorrel	*Rumex acetosa*

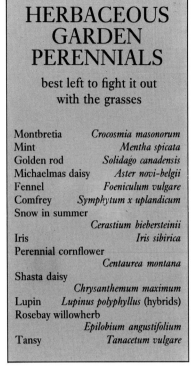

HERBACEOUS GARDEN PERENNIALS

best left to fight it out
with the grasses

Montbretia	*Crocosmia masonorum*
Mint	*Mentha spicata*
Golden rod	*Solidago canadensis*
Michaelmas daisy	*Aster novi-belgii*
Fennel	*Foeniculum vulgare*
Comfrey	*Symphytum x uplandicum*
Snow in summer	
	Cerastium biebersteinii
Iris	*Iris sibirica*
Perennial cornflower	
	Centaurea montana
Shasta daisy	
	Chrysanthemum maximum
Lupin	*Lupinus polyphyllus* (hybrids)
Rosebay willowherb	
	Epilobium angustifolium
Tansy	*Tanacetum vulgare*

wildflower seedlings through the grass and into the soil. With this technique the wildflowers are already well established, and they are able to compete from the start.

The other two techniques are really variations on the same theme. They involve sowing seed, but making a way through the tight-knit grass sward first, to allow the seed access to the soil. The first method is scarifying, or ripping the turf. On a small scale you can use a garden rake, but for a real park meadow you are better using a spiked harrow, mounted on a tractor and weighted. The spikes tear at the surface, and when seed is thinly sown on top, some of it manages to get down through the grass. The other variation on this theme is to use a weedkiller, and this is something which really must be left to the trained experts in the parks department. There are special selective weedkillers which will kill grasses and leave broad-leaved weeds unharmed. This is quite the opposite of the normal routine when a completely different range of weedkiller is used to kill the daisies and dandelions and keep the grass. If the turf is sprayed with grasskiller, then again the soil between the broad-leaved weeds is exposed and wildflower seed can be successfully oversown.

There is now a sort of combination of the two techniques available. An agricultural machine is used which can inject seed into the soil, whilst at the same time squirting a total weedkiller on the turf where the seed has been sown. The turf dies in the area of the squirt, and the seedling wildflower is then able to establish itself relatively free from competition. This technique is very successful, but only really if you sow seed of a single species. The various meadow wildflowers have seed of a whole range of different sizes and shapes, and if you mix them then the seeds tend to clog up the machine. Of course, you must also ask yourself whether or not it is a good idea to use chemicals to improve wildlife habitat.

There are relatively few opportunities in parks for sowing new meadows, but there is a chance to start from scratch with new road verges, for example, or the grassland around new office blocks. Here the golden rule is to avoid using topsoil. This is far too fertile and full of weed-seed to give the wildflowers a chance. Persuade the council's engineers to spread a sandy subsoil over well-drained ground, and then sow it very thinly with a mixture of fine grasses and just one or two easy wildflowers. The seedsmen are very fond of producing mixtures with twenty or thirty different species in them, but quite honestly most of them don't survive, and

in any case, it is colour and beauty that are going to please people, and persuade them it is a good idea. Once they are won over by a successful sheet of ox-eye daisy, scabious and buttercup, then you can think about introducing more unusual species which might increase insect diversity or extend the flowering season. Reputable seedsmen will all offer you expert advice, and produce a range of mixtures for specific soil types, for wet or dry land, and for spring or summer cutting. Take that advice, but take it with a pinch of salt, and if in doubt, reduce the amount of seed, and limit the range of species. Once you get the habitat and the management sorted out, it is surprising how quickly new species seem to arrive and settle in. A very thin sowing will leave plenty of gaps, and plenty of room for incomers.

Why shouldn't children be able to pick daisies in the park? How sad that we use our technology to kill wildflowers. It would be so easy to provide perfect blooms for everyone to make a daisy chain.

There are problems with wildflower meadows in towns of course. If it was that easy they would be much more common than they are. First of all, it is not nearly so quick or easy to cut grass eighteen inches high, as it is to mow over a patch that was cut only ten days earlier. It needs different kinds of machines, and these may not be available, or they may not be able to negotiate the obstacles in a park. Long grass is a fire-risk, too, and with a lot more people using the parks there is a serious problem with cigarette ends, or even deliberate burning. Here, yet again, a close-mown margin can help increase respect

Long grass also has a tendency to accumulate and then hide junk. Supermarket trolleys are a favourite, abandoned after a race around the park. It is not so funny when the mower hits the trolley, though, and all cutting stops for a week whilst the machine is repaired.

NATIVE GRASSES

Less aggressive species
with 'pretty' flowers

Creeping bent	*Agrostis stolonifera*
Browntop	*Agrostis tenuis*
Meadow foxtail	*Alopecuris pratensis*
Sweet vernal	
	Anthoxanthum odoratum
Crested dogstail	*Cynosurus cristatus*
Red fescue	*Festuca rubra*
Yorkshire fog	*Holcus lanatus*
Timothy	*Phleum pratense*
Smooth meadow grass	
	Poa pratensis
Quaking grass	*Briza media*

The difficulties don't end when the hay is cut either. For the past fifty years parks managers have been striving to reduce to a minimum the peaks of labour required in a park. That is why labour-intensive spring-bedding is such a rarity now. In the middle of the holiday period when the labour force is already stretched to breaking point, patrolling from dawn till dusk, mowing road verges and playing fields once a fortnight and generally coping with 'the busy season' the idea of coping with municipal haymaking will go down like a lead balloon in the average parks office. This is where *you* come in. The vision of parks staff in smocks and straw hats, complete with jugs of cider, may well be out of the question, though in Holland the parks department do take on seasonal labour for just this kind of work. That image of traditional haymaking is a marvellous one to capture the imagination and enthusiasm of local people. Community haymaking parties really can work. Choose a couple of weekends in early July. Let as many people as possible know, and then ask for the parks staff to mow just a week earlier. Such a genuinely helpful offer of physical assistance is bound to have them co-operating in no time. The hay needs turning the first weekend, and then raking up and carting away the second. There will be plenty of small-scale takers for the hay itself – with every hamster and guinea pig for miles around spending the rest of the year in clover, so to speak, and there are a growing number of city farms too, with goats and rabbits, and even cows willing and able to make use of a nice tasty crop of organically grown herb-rich hay. If yours is a school hay meadow, then you can obviously adjust the mowing regime to give you annual haymaking either in the doldrums just before the long summer break, or as a further boost to the fun of the new autumn term.

If the hay meadow is big enough, then it is quite realistic to expect a farmer or an agricultural contractor to cut and remove the hay crop. Only in exceptional circumstances would there be much money changing hands, but at least grass which was previously both boring and costly will now be attractive, interesting and free to maintain. The one thing to watch out for with this commercial arrangement is the timing of the cut. Apparently there is an economic advantage in cutting slightly early, to get the maximum energy content in the hay. From our point of view, though, the hay must be left standing long enough for wildflowers to set ripe seed, and that means delaying the operation a little. It is best to

license the hay cutting on an annual basis too. Any agreement
for more than one year and you run the risk of establishing
an 'agricultural tenancy', irrevocable for three generations.

Once the hay has been harvested, the grass continues to
grow, and this so-called 'aftermath' can get quite long by
the autumn. In smaller parks, this is where a September
tidy-up cut is useful, to remove the secondary growth before
the winter. In the traditional meadows of the countryside, that
aftermath would have provided a valuable grazing crop for
winter cattle or sheep, and the trampling of their hooves
undoubtedly helped push in the freshly fallen wildflower
seed and maintain the wildlife community. Grazing in town
meadows is not such a silly idea, and it is catching on in
more and more parks departments. Sheep are generally
unsuitable, since they are liable to be worried by town dogs, or
rustled by midnight cowboys, though they are being used
successfully in the genteel town squares of Bath. Certainly
cattle, ponies and deer are all being used effectively and here
again is another way of increasing interest within the park
whilst reducing mowing costs. Deer are really an
all-year-round commitment, and when they are used it is
generally to continue a long deer-park tradition. Horses and
ponies are a readily available kind of grazing stock in towns.
Winter grazing, in particular, is always in short supply, but
pasture grazed by horses tends to be very messy: the public
will want to come and feed them, which concentrates the
trampling damage they do, and horses also have the habit
of manuring in one or two favourite latrine areas. This quickly
boosts the fertility, and not surprisingly the animals tend to
avoid grazing these patches too. The result is a very scruffy
paddock, with mud around the gates, and great clumps of
nettles and docks in the enriched corners: not a pretty
landscape at all.

Cattle are probably the best bet for grazing city meadows.
They can be bought and sold at market easily, can hold their
own against the odd rogue Alsatian, and they do graze to
produce a reasonably flowery meadow. They look attractive,
too, and confirm that countryside atmosphere. You are rather
stuck with bullocks or heifers, since milking cows are
obviously far too much trouble, and bulls are definitely a bad
idea. The best breed of all seems to be Highland cattle.
They may look ferocious, but are in fact exceptionally docile
and they are also tough enough to withstand outdoor winter
living. The breeds to avoid are Jerseys and Guernseys,

apparently. Behind those big brown eyes there lurks a pretty vicious temperament.

If you do persuade the parks department to try grazing livestock, then there are certain special arrangements that have to be made. The animals will need access to drinking water, for example, and they will need some of that famous hay to eat in snowy weather. Perhaps most importantly they will need to be kept securely in one place. Generally that means fencing, to protect the rest of the park, and prevent total chaos in the High Street, but for small scale grazing, when linked to a city farm, for instance, it may be quite realistic to tether individual animals, and return them to the shelter of the farm 'buildings' each evening. Grazing animals do mean making special provision for people too. For every child who is crazy about horses, or frantic to feed the cows, there will be another alienated city-dweller who is terrified of the things. It must remain perfectly possible to walk in the park without coming face to face with a frisky herd of bullocks.

One other animal which grazes a surprising number of our city parks already is the goose. If there is a lake in the park, then generally there will be a thriving flock of Canada geese, and whilst they may fly noisily to meet anyone who shows the slightest sign of being a crust-carrier, they are essentially grazing birds. There is an area of grass beside the lake in Cannon Hill Park, Birmingham, which is grazed this way. I say 'grass', but in fact it has become a monoculture of daisies since the geese moved in. They graze off any blade of grass that dares to appear, and all those wet webbed feet seem to make sure that the only plant able to stand the conditions is the daisy. There are other lakeside grasslands I can think of where the geese are not so numerous – less bread available, I imagine – and here the grazing birds do a very good job of keeping the grass cropped short. Over-grazing is a problem you would not normally find in the wild. The geese would simply move over a wider area. Towns are different, though. In this case the crusts of bread compound the problem, and the high population of ducks, geese and swans this creates makes it very difficult for wetland species in general to survive. Reed-beds and other water plants are eaten as soon as they are planted, and tadpoles, dragonflies and any other species that move are snapped up in no time by greedy wildfowl of one sort or another. There is a more positive side to wetland habitat in towns, though, and that is the subject I'll tackle next.

The thinking man's mowing machine?

URBAN WETLANDS

9

My very earliest memory of play was sitting on the draining board, with my feet in the kitchen sink, 'ladling and teeming' water. Long before I was old enough for school, I remember taking great delight in splashing through the puddles in my wellies, and certainly most of my earliest wildlife thrills were by the waterside. How often do you see children, still in pushchairs, giggling as they feed bread to the ducks around the park lake?

One of the essential achievements of early childhood is to succeed in catching tiddlers and tadpoles to put proudly into a jam jar, and what about the joy of managing to send a pebble skimming successfully across the ripple of the local pond? I spent hours as a child building dams in tiny, trickling streams, and was amused years later to see a specially constructed 'mountain stream' in Amsterdam. This was a

People and ducks go naturally together, but this isn't my idea of the ideal water-edge. We can do much better than a sharp, sterile, concrete margin.

This is much better. It is still a park lake, but the edges are shallow, with plenty of natural vegetation, and people have much more of a 'wetland experience'.

WATER PLANTS

These grow best with their roots in shallow-water. Plant at the edge of ponds and lakes.

Water plantain	
	Alisma plantago-aquatica
Fools watercress	*Apium nodiflorum*
Flowering rush*	*Butomus umbellatus*
Water mint	*Mentha aquatica*
Bogbean*	*Menyanthes trifoliata*
Water forget-me-not	
	Myosotis scorpioides
Amphibious bistort*	
	Polygonum amphibium
Lesser spearwort*	
	Ranunculus flammula
Greater spearwort	
	Ranunculus lingua
Great water dock	
	Rumex hydrolapathum
Arrowhead	
	Sagittaria sagittifolia
Unbranched bur-reed	
	Sparganium emersum
Branched bur-reed	
	Sparganium erectum
Lesser reedmace	*Typha angustifolia*
Reedmace (bulrush)	*Typha latifolia*
Common reed	*Phragmites australis*
Brooklime*	*Veronica beccabunga*

* less aggressive, small-growing species.

highly successful play feature in the 1982 Garden Festival. Trickling streams are unheard of in that flat part of the Netherlands, but given a pump, an artificial slope and a pile of stones, those Dutch children knew exactly what to do. They were happily building dams and waterfalls, exactly as I had done years before.

Our wildlife has more than a passing interest in water, too. Apart from the obvious need for all plants and animals to take in water in order to survive, there is a huge number of species which are actually dependent upon wetlands as a vital part of their habitat. Many of our prettiest wildflowers, for example, need to grow with their roots in the waterlogged soil of the water's edge. Flag irises, ragged robin, marsh-marigold, brooklime and bulrush are just a few of the plants that depend upon wetness, whilst water-lilies, pondweeds, bogbean and several others actually grow up through the water itself.

Water provides a suitable environment for many species of animals to breed. Fish live there throughout their lives, of course, and we have a marvellous range of freshwater species in our ponds, rivers and lakes, from tiny minnows to huge pike and carp. Our amphibians use water for breeding, with frogs, newts and toads all returning in early spring to spawn, before wandering back to the wet grasses and damp logs for feeding and hibernation. Most unpolluted water is teeming with invertebrate life of one sort or another. There are big creatures such as pond snails, but there is a real soup of smaller creatures too, all in water for part of their lives, and many of them changing from strange little wriggly things into elegant winged insects, and flying away to find new wetlands, a momentary mate, and a suitable site where they themselves can breed.

Britain's wetlands are not simply of local interest either. Our bogs and marshes, ponds, lakes, rivers and streams are the biggest contribution we make to wildlife and conservation on a world scale. These islands are quite peculiar in forming such an important terminus for international bird migration. Some species travel here to enjoy our grasslands – the corncrake in summer, and the starlings in winter, for example. Many of our visitors are woodland birds – chiffchaffs and willow warblers, nightingales and flycatchers in summer, and siskins, redpoll, and a whole mass of seed and fruit-eaters in the winter. Migrant wetland species are undoubtedly the most spectacular, however, and probably the ones most at

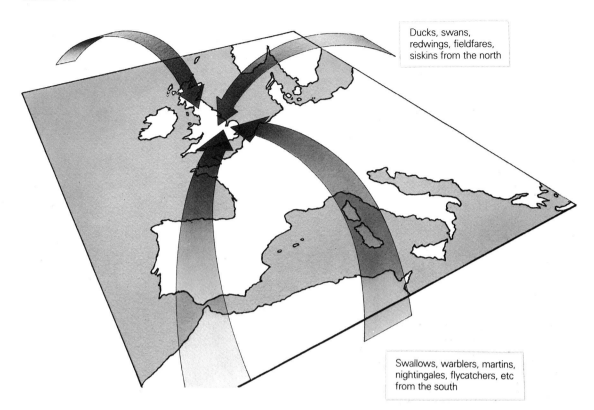

Ducks, swans,
redwings, fieldfares,
siskins from the north

Swallows, warblers, martins,
nightingales, flycatchers, etc
from the south

risk. Some of the ducks you feed around the park lake may well have flown south for the winter from Scandinavia or even Greenland. We play host to hundreds of thousands of ducks, swans, geese and waders from the north each year and all of them are here to 'take the waters'. We have summer visitors to our wetlands, too. Warblers weave their nests into the growing stems of waterside reeds, whilst swallows and house martins gather wet mud to build theirs.

With so much public love of the waterside, and so much international responsibility for wetland habitat, it is depressing to discover how much of it we have destroyed in recent years. Of course we have been draining land for centuries. King John turned the swamps of Avalon into the rich wet-pastures of the Somerset levels over seven centuries ago. Much of East Anglia was reed-bed and swamp until the sixteenth century, when drainage and water-pumping technology were introduced from the Netherlands. The wetlands of Britain have grown smaller and drier over the centuries, and the species that depend on them have become less and less common. Now, quite suddenly, the situation has reached crisis pitch. Species such as the booming bittern,

Millions of birds migrate to and from north-west Europe. Britain is a terminus for birds from Africa in the summer and from Scandinavia, Greenland and northern Russia in the winter.

which must once have been quite common, have been on the brink of extinction for generations, and just manage to cling on in two or three very wet, reedy places. Ironically, they are probably safer now than at any time this century, simply because they are so rare that their plight is taken seriously. The 'crisis' is to do with the common wetland species. The common frog which everyone took so much for granted has dropped in number by over 90% in ten years in many lowland farming counties. The great crested newt, seen by many a small child in the recent past as their only familiar, accessible, catchable prehistoric monster, is on the endangered species list for Europe, and is 'protected' by international law. Wonderful wetland wildflowers such as ragged robin, greater spearwort and flowering rush have become rare, threatened species within my lifetime. Salmon stocks are so depleted in many of their traditional spawning rivers that the whole economy of certain sporting areas is threatened. We have dragonfly species on the brink of extinction, and one or two which have actually gone. All in all, the common wildlife of our wetland habitats is in very real danger.

Whilst the emerging towns were responsible for a great deal of the wetland habitat loss in the last century, it is farming intensification which has finally brought the crisis to a head in recent years. With modern machinery it is so easy to fill in a pond, pipe a ditch or drain a marsh, and with a guaranteed and generous price for intensively produced crops, farmers have taken over control of the drainage boards in most of England and Wales, and spent billions of public pounds wrecking streams and rivers in order to make field drainage possible, and crop subsidies claimable. Such sympathetic farming practices as water meadow management have disappeared completely in the past fifty years, and any wetland which does still remain is either a gesture of extreme generosity on the part of the farmer, or a sign of a landowner who has failed to make the most of the financial subsidy bonanza. The Ministry of Agriculture has offered huge incentives to drain land, in order to increase production yet again. Even when a wetland has actually managed to remain wet, it is not necessarily safe. The other major assault of British agriculture is chemical pollution, and a great many wetlands and watercourses are currently being killed by fertiliser run-off and pesticide spray.

The last great hope for the survival of British wetland wildlife is the towns. Strict pollution control should mean

Frogs are (almost) everybody's favourite – but their numbers in the countryside have dropped by 90% in ten years. Ponds and ditches are almost a thing of the past, but there is plenty of scope for more frog-habitat in towns.

that there is less and less risk of chemical damage, but there is also great scope for creating extensive new wetland habitats within the safety of the city, and the one good thing about wetlands is that they are quick to recover, and relatively easy to start from scratch. Remember those mining flashes we talked about earlier. Some of the wildest are less than thirty years old, and since much wetland wildlife is extremely mobile with floating seeds, swimming fry and flying insects and birds all able to move around from one wet habitat to the next, new wetlands can easily be created, and with a bit of skill, and a following wind, we could still save this part of our natural heritage.

Almost every town and city in Britain owes its origins, at least in part, to a stream or river. The very earliest settlements were often at fording places, or the head of navigation where boats were forced to unload. For hundreds of years, water was our main source of power, with cornmills drawing in people from the surrounding countryside, and establishing the basis of a village or a market town. My own childhood was spent in the Rivelin Valley, on the southern edge of Sheffield, and here, as in so many industrial cities, it was the river's power which paved the way for the dirtier, noisier, coal-based industrial revolution. The Rivelin was dammed and diverted a score of times within its few short miles, to create tilt-ponds which drove water-wheels, grindstones and tilt hammers. This was the origin of Sheffield's cutlery trade, and the goods produced by that little river's power were exported worldwide.

Now I live in the West Midlands, and again I am surrounded by old millponds. Many of them silted up long ago and are willowy, wet or wooded nowadays. Here the locals used the water-power for scythe making, and to temper sword blades, and so the streams and rivers of South Staffordshire established the settlements which were eventually to become the 'endless village' of the Black Country.

Once coal and steam arrived, the smaller watercourses became redundant as a source of power, though the bigger rivers continued to provide the transport system for barges of coal and ironstone. Towns and cities expanded dramatically, and the streams that for generations had been the centre of the settlement were suddenly abandoned and lost behind blackened factories and terraced houses. There was a brief moment when canals were built to extend the river transport system, allowing fuel and raw materials to reach riverless settlements, and this man-made network gave life to new boom cities such as Birmingham. Canal transport was short-lived, however, and when the railway age arrived, even the grandest of our rivers were relegated to the role of sewer. For almost two hundred years, most of our lowland rivers were virtually dead. The river Tawe in Swansea was possibly the worst of all. This valley led the world in metal smelting, and the combined forces of copper, arsenic, lead, zinc and numerous other heavy metals led to the total devastation of all life in that once rich river.

The Tawe may have been the worst, but there was little to choose between the dozens of urban rivers until the middle of this century. In fact many of our rivers remained polluted to death until the early seventies, when at last a real effort was made to begin cleaning them up. The Thames is the most celebrated success story. This great river is now the cleanest it has been for perhaps five hundred years. Industrial pollution is controlled; most urban sewage is properly treated, and at last, the river is supporting a rich variety of wildlife. Anglers have caught well over one hundred species of fresh water and brackish estuarine fish. Even salmon are returning annually to spawn. In fact, aquatic life has now recovered so well that those trapped fish are causing a blockage problem in the inlet grilles of several power stations. There are flocks of waders such as redshank, dunlin and the occasional solitary heron to be seen feeding on the mud-banks by the Houses of Parliament, and the evil smell which dominated Thamesside London for centuries is now just a faint, unpleasant memory.

Other river clear-ups are not so far advanced. The Mersey, for instance, is still heavily polluted by what little industry is managing to survive, and with such economic difficulties it is not surprising that the polluters are pleading poverty and failing to clean up their act for fear of final collapse. In time, with help from the public purse, I expect even this great river will be clean again, and the wildlife will return.

Lowland rivers flood. This is quite natural, and in the countryside it used to help produce some of our most valuable wildlife habitat. The water-covered 'silver-meadows' of the river flood plain were rich feeding grounds for winter wildfowl, and the fertile silt this process deposits on the riverside pastures, coupled with the warming effect of an insulating layer of water during the icy months of February and March, helped make water-meadows some of our most highly prized grazing lands. For centuries, farmers flooded the riverside

Vast amounts of public money are poured into brutalising river banks. With proper care the drainage engineer can avoid this kind of devastation, and even improve the wildlife corridor.

It is safer in the shallows. Fluffy little coot chicks can escape predators, the water is warmer, and there are more little wriggly things to eat.

pasture every winter, to give themselves an 'early bite' of spring grazing. In recent years, the flooding of farmland has come to be seen as 'inefficient' since winter wheat and sugar beet have been made artificially more rewarding than an early bite of grass.

In the town, flooding has never been 'a good thing' and so as industrial settlements grew, the increasingly polluted streams and rivers were dealt a second devastating blow as their beds were lowered, their banks were walled in, and they were transformed from rich ribbons of silver and green into sterile stone-lined ditches, devoid of any kind of wildlife shelter. The problem of flooding was also aggravated by the towns themselves. A rainstorm or a snow-melt in the countryside takes days to soak, seep and trickle its way through the soft, green landscape to the streams and rivers, and this spreads the flood-load considerably. In a town, the rain falls not on absorbent green fields, but on slate roofs, tarmac roads and concrete yards. It is whisked away down drainpipes, gutters and sewers and is swelling the hard-pressed rivers within minutes. This makes water-levels rise alarmingly and seems always to be met with the predictable response of even deeper channels, higher stone banks and further sterilisation. All 'inconvenient' waterside habitat is removed, to minimise the risk of a blockage, and there is almost nowhere left for wildlife to live.

With so much pressure to contain urban waterways, and prevent flooding at all costs, the surprising thing is that, even in the grimiest of cities, there are still stretches of riverbank which are green and leafy. Where industrial buildings have, for some reason, not crowded in quite so closely, there are willows, and grassy banks, clumps of alder, and perhaps even marsh marigolds to add a splash of spring colour. Now that the water is becoming cleaner, there are dragonflies and moorhens in these leafy little interludes. Water voles have returned to burrow amongst the tree roots, and there is just a glimpse of the delights our urban rivers could provide, if we can find ways of undoing the damage caused by our brutal, greedy, filthy recent past. The good news is that spectacular improvements are fast becoming a reality.

People in towns pay twice for the often insensitive treatment of their rivers. Through water rates we fund the drainage authorities, and although the vast majority of their income comes from town-dwellers, most of the work they do goes on in the farming countryside. This leaves town drainage relatively neglected, and so the bulk of the work on our urban rivers is carried out by local councils, paid for a second time through the city rates.

Since we are paying twice over, every one of us has the right to insist that the work done by our engineers is sensitive, sensible, and of benefit to the river's wildlife. This may seem a daunting task, faced with the army of bureaucrats and authoritative technologists, but it can be done. The simple fact is that engineers have rarely been asked to do anything but create super-efficient, sterile ditches until now. Challenge them to carry out their essential drainage improvement

This is one of the last bits of Birmingham's River Rea to be left 'unimproved', and it makes ideal habitat for wildlife and for the local kids.

whilst at the same time creating or conserving river cliffs for
kingfisher nests, overhanging trees for mallard, reed-beds
for moorhen and dragonfly, spawning grounds for fish, shingle
banks for waders, and all the other intricate details which make
up a living stream or river. Ask, and you may find that those
self-same engineers rise to the challenge, and begin redirecting
their energy, their skill and their huge amounts of public
money towards a drainage system which combines efficiency
with beauty and richness of habitat. Remember that it is much
easier to produce a mindless concrete channel. That brutal
solution doesn't demand any thinking time, but our waterways
are far too precious to be 'thrown away' for lack of
imagination. It is our pressure, as simple rate-paying members
of the public, which will stimulate our engineers and elected
politicians to start bothering about quality in our rivers, as
well as quantity.

The River Rea was known as 'the Mother of Birmingham'
because, small though it is, it supported numerous water mills,
and helped found Brum's industrial heritage. That working
history is still evident in local names. This little river has a
very urban address, flowing from the Longbridge car factory
in the south to Spaghetti Junction in the north, and although
there are stretches of it, in the leafier suburbs, which are still
delightfully wild, the city council has a policy of
'improvement', which is relentlessly canalising the Rea, by
pouring £200,000 every year into straightening, deepening
and devastating. There are kingfishers on the Rea, and there
is even one small stretch of wet riverbank, within the safety
of a private factory's security fence, where wild daffodils grow,
but with each year that passes more and more of the lovely
little river is devastated by machines, concrete and highly paid
brutal ignorance. The Urban Wildlife Group, prompted by
a few of the nature-lovers who live by the Rea, began
suggesting to the city council that there was an alternative,
more sensitive way of improving the Rea. We began by
explaining the river's importance as one of those vital corridors
which bring wildlife into the heart of the city, and connect
with other ribbons of green along the canals and railway
embankments. The councillors listened. We then gave them
precise, positive suggestions, and began to encourage the
engineers to think about new ways of working. Whole books
have since been written on 'conservation and river
engineering', but this was the kind of simple thing we
suggested. First of all, we said that there should be a much

more detailed survey of the surviving stretches of river. This was something we knew local people could do, and it would prove to the engineers that there really was something there worth saving. Most of the habitat which had been lost so far had been destroyed in complete ignorance of its value. Once the old willow trees, the river cliffs, the waterfalls and so on were identified as 'valuable', there was a need to find ways of caring for them. Of course we realised that some things would have to go, but many of the trees, for instance, were chopped down simply to allow a dredging machine access to the stream itself. With careful planning, the machine could often work from one bank only, and leave the trees on the other bank undamaged. In fact the engineers agreed that the tree roots did a valuable job of holding the bank together, and we hung on to our nesting sites for wrens, wagtails and other creatures of the riverbank.

Where silt was dredged out it was all too often dumped on valuable riverside vegetation, piled up around the base of nearby trees, or used to fill in wet hollows or stream-side pools. This destruction was quite unnecessary, and simply needed a little more thought. At this level it was the machine drivers who needed to be converted to our ideas, rather than the engineers, and it really came as no surprise to find that they were very sympathetic – even enthusiastic – and began thinking of exciting new ways to exploit their great skill with a machine and create new habitat features as an integral part of their drainage work. The idea that, by creating a shallow shelf of silt in a widened stretch of stream, they would be providing a home for flag iris, arrowhead and a whole range of riverside animal life really did excite them, and they took great delight in inventing new habitat details as a part of their working day.

Now, just two or three years after we first began to criticise, there is a positive move to employ those huge sums of money creatively, to enrich this one small example of an urban river corridor, create new habitats, and develop the Rea as a positive asset for the local community and its wildlife, rather than the degraded, lifeless drain it was in danger of becoming.

The most exciting breakthrough of all has come with the realisation that river flooding can be managed and directed rather than simply suppressed. There is room now in our hollowed out, post-industrial towns and cities to allow urban rivers to burst their banks once more and flood the surrounding land. This cannot simply be allowed to happen at random, of course. People would drown. There is, however, an increasing realisation that land can be set aside for flood control, where the winter torrents can be diverted and allowed to rest before trickling gently back into the mainstream once the deluge is over. Such flood-control lagoons tend on the whole to be treated as sterile overflow areas, and carpeted with yet more close-mown rye-grass desert. With imagination they can become immensely valuable wetland habitats, and add considerably to the urban wildlife network.

It is a relatively simple thing for an engineer to build a 'bottleneck' into a stream or river, so that in times of flood the water backs up, and overflows the banks, flooding the adjacent land. This work is happening anyway. On just one small river – this time the Tame, in the Black Country – there are three such schemes within as many miles. The engineering work for each cost about one million pounds in the early 1980s, but in wildlife terms the results differ greatly. The first is a simple sheet of close-mown grass, dry at all times except for the two or three days immediately following a flood. Nothing lives here but grass and daisies, the odd roosting seagull and an occasional passing flock of starlings.

The second flood area is quite different. This time the lagoon is permanently wet, and the water level simply rises temporarily during floods. The engineers have worked closely with professional conservationists, particularly from the Royal Society for the Protection of Birds, and the money they spent has yielded the bonus of a wonderful new nature reserve. There is marshland, permanently waterlogged, where I have watched snipe feeding, and even enjoyed fine views of a hen-harrier quartering the golden reed-bed, in search of small birds. There is wet grassland too, churned up a little by grazing ponies, where as many as sixteen herons have been seen, standing motionless, and just occasionally lungeing forward to catch a frog, or some other poor unfortunate wetland creature. Part of this floodland reserve is maintained as open water, with islands to provide safe nesting sites, and in the winter months hundreds of ducks and geese of various species gather here. In fact the lake has become so popular with the wildfowl that the RSPB are having great difficulty growing the waterside plants that would complete the habitat. Again it is a bread-based problem. The bird population is boosted by kind visitors to the other end of the lake, beyond the control of the RSPB. When the bread runs out, the birds turn their attention to anything else which is edible, and this usually means a mass migration into the bird reserve, where everything green is razed to the ground.

The third overflow lagoon is largely made up of lakes, and although these will eventually form part of a public park, they have been designed for wildlife, and are being kept 'under wraps' until the vegetation is established.

You may well be wondering what on earth you can do as an individual to help create wetland habitat at this large scale. Again the answer lies partly in the need to press for change. You should be writing to your drainage authority and your local council, but there are practical things you can do, too. At the passive level, there is a need for people to keep records of the wildlife which uses the new habitats. If you have time on your hands, you could help increase the strength of the argument for more new wetland, by watching the habitat regularly, and so showing the politicians and engineers in particular that there really is a build-up of new wildlife thanks to their efforts. A wet pasture in Kent showed a ten-fold increase in snipe over three winters, simply because the ground was made more waterlogged. With every week that passes, the RSPB warden on the Tame clocks up new additions to the bird list.

Birds are easy. They are big, and relatively easy to see, but it is the development of insect populations, and particularly the establishment of wetland wildflowers, that really shows how valuable the work can be.

There are a number of very practical ways in which you can help to fine-tune the habitat, once the engineers have done their work. Ideally, they will have left you wetland with a varied depth of water, and a wavy-edged shoreline. Much of the animal life you hope to attract is very territorial, and the more inlets and promontories you can offer, the greater will be the number of defensible territories, and so the population of nesting coots, breeding dragonflies and spawning fish will be increased.

You may have islands provided by the engineer, but if not, then it can be great fun building them as floating rafts, and then anchoring them at a safe distance from the shore. Be sure to build them strongly, with a welded metal frame if possible, and buoyancy provided by blocks of polystyrene or sealed drums. Build in planting boxes which allow you to grow clumps of reeds as camouflage, and then you will almost certainly have your floating island adopted as a nest site. Mallard are probably the most likely tenants, though they seem to prefer some kind of shelter. If the lake is big enough, then Canada geese will often nest on board. Coots are frequent takers, and if you are really lucky you may have the beautiful great-crested grebe as a resident. If you have room, try making one or two islands which are kept free of vegetation, and covered instead with coarse gravel. These may be adopted by the delightful little ringed plover, or in very special circumstances you may even establish a tern colony.

Obviously the construction of a floating island is quite an ambitious project, but it makes an ideal summer holiday task for an energetic group of youngsters, or perhaps for a fishing club with time on their hands during the closed season. You will need permission, probably from the drainage authority, but they shouldn't object unless your lake forms part of the drinking water supply, and they are anxious about pollution.

The habitat below water is just as important as that at the surface. After all, most of the more obvious large-scale wildlife that you enjoy watching from the waterside is feeding on either insect larvae or fish. One quite novel idea which has worked very well in the reservoirs of North America, is the building of artificial reefs on the lake bed, to provide breeding and hiding habitat for aquatic creatures. All kinds of materials have been used, from scrap railway carriages and trolley buses to wrecked cars. The material I would

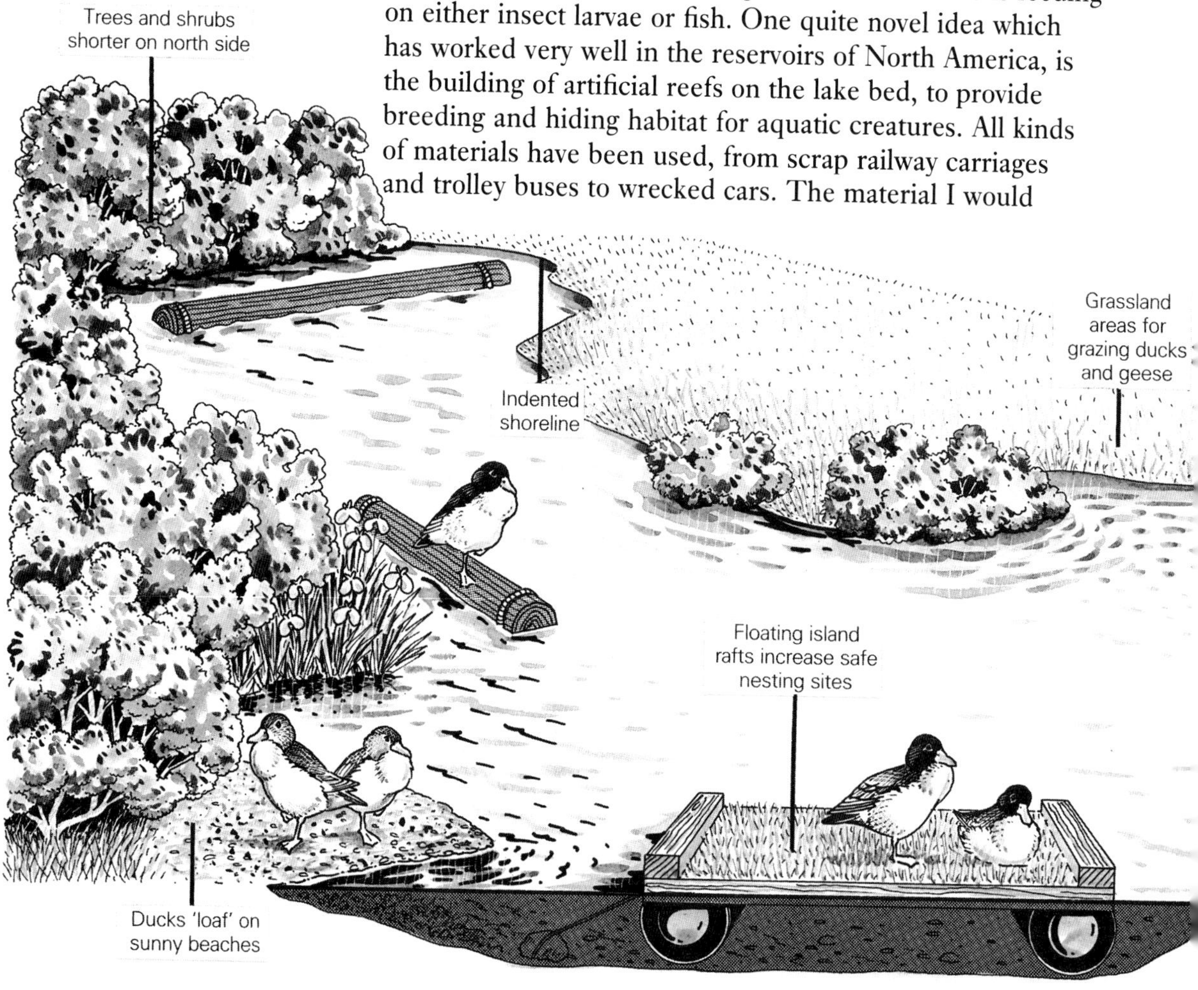

Trees and shrubs shorter on north side

Grassland areas for grazing ducks and geese

Indented shoreline

Floating island rafts increase safe nesting sites

Ducks 'loaf' on sunny beaches

recommend for use here is worn car and lorry tyres. These
are a growing menace in much of the landscape, and they are
relatively easy to float into position, and then to sink
permanently by splashing them to shake out the trapped air
bubbles, or by puncturing the walls of the tyres. If you get
the chance to work in the dry bed of a new lake before it is
flooded, then you can build whole underwater cities of tyres,
with lots of holes and tunnels to hide in, but if you're involved
after the water is there, just float them out, sink them and
hope for the best.

You can help establish the waterside plant life, too. The
critical thing is to make sure there is shallow water, since
very little can grow in water more than ten feet deep, and most
of the so-called 'emergent' plants such as bulrush, spearwort
and flag iris need water much shallower than that. The planting
should be carried out in April or early May, when the leaves
have begun to grow. Generally, you will be able to obtain
suitable plants from another pond, canal or riverbank where
things have become overgrown and clearance work is taking
place. (Contact your local conservation volunteers to find
out where this kind of work is going on.) This will give you
clumps of soil and roots, and the problem is how to stop
them floating to the surface when you stick them down on the
bed of your lake. The easiest solution to the problem is to
wrap each clump of rootstock in a piece of sacking or an old
vegetable net weighted with a stone or two, tie it securely,
and then lob it out into the shallows where it will sink to the
bottom. Check in which depth of water the plant normally
grows, and try to find a similar depth for your new planting.

Floating 'booms' reduce
wave action and help marginal
plants to establish

Shrub cover allows timid
wildlife safe access

Old car tyres can be used
to make an artificial reef

The other problem you may need to overcome is that of wave action. It is surprising what powers of erosion build up in the ripples on even a small sheet of water. Once your vegetation is established, that in itself will break up the wave action and reduce the damage, but the problem is actually getting plants started. The answer is to tether some kind of floating 'boom' a little way out from the shoreline. Pieces of floating timber will do, or even a string of plastic bottles. These will help break up the waves, and so create a kind of miniature reef which allows the plants to grow safely in the still water lagoons within.

It takes quite a bit of organising to be able to have a real input into expensive flood control schemes. You can imagine that engineers and politicians with hundreds of thousands of pounds to spend do sometimes get a bit possessive about their projects. For most of us, a much more achievable target is that boring old concrete-edged lake in the local park. It may well have plenty of ducks to fight over your crusts of bread, but most of these lakes are pretty hostile when it comes to any other kind of wildlife, and they could be wonderful. Many parks departments regard their redundant boating lakes as a bit of a liability, so any suggestion for improving them should be welcomed. Get them to begin by filling in part of the lake, to create an area of shallow water, preferably on the sunny side, where reeds and other wetland plants can grow happily, and where animal life can pass safely in and out of water. Almost anything that isn't chemically poisonous can be used to create the shallows. Demolition rubble is ideal, but you could use those old tyres again, topped off with subsoil or gravel. Create one or two tongues of shallow water and if you then plant them with emergent waterside plants, you will quickly develop a habitat for a wider variety of water-life. If you expect to have problems from the ducks, try stretching a sheet of netting just above the surface of the water. The plants will grow through, but the birds will have difficulty raiding the area. Suggest a reduction in artificial feeding, too, to keep the bird numbers down, at least until the plants are established.

If you are looking for success in breeding fish and ducklings, then research has shown that safe, sheltered shallows close to shore are a great help. Many ducklings die, for instance, because their fluffy down becomes waterlogged, and they get very cold. Shallows are warmer. Some ducklings, and a great many young fish fry, fall prey to predators, and a nice,

weedy, shallow margin provides safe escape for the babies –
particularly from predatory pike.

Angling itself can create a conflict with wildlife
conservation, but it is a major recreational pastime for
millions of people, and therefore it is best to cater for it
positively. Provide convenient, accessible fishing platforms
around certain stretches of shoreline, and you can then
reasonably expect the anglers to keep clear of the
conservation shoreline elsewhere. The fishing 'pegs'
concentrate the pressure very well, and you will find there
is much less wearing away of the plants between the platforms
as a result. It is in the interest of fishing to have conservation
sanctuary areas where fish can breed in safety and find natural
food, and of course fishing clubs are often enthusiastic about
carrying out conservation work, particularly outside the fishing
season. It is worth encouraging some kind of licence for
fishing. This will allow for certain rules to be established, and
it should be possible to prevent litter, and particularly to ban
the use of lead weights, and the irresponsible dropping of line
and hooks. Carelessness by anglers is now known to be
responsible for the painful death of thousands of ducks, swans
and geese every year and a few simple rules will allow anglers
and wildlife to live happily side by side. For a long time, the
alternatives to lead fishing weights have been pretty useless,
but recent developments have produced a form of tungsten-
based weight which comes in the form of a thin, flexible tube
which can be cut to length. This seems to be both efficient
and safe, but the fishing community are a pretty conservative
lot, and are unlikely to stop using lead until they are made to.

When it comes to creating successful habitat for migratory
wildfowl and waders, success depends a great deal on where
you are. The birds follow traditional migration routes, crossing
the Channel and North Sea at particular points, and
returning to specific wintering grounds year after year. This
is one reason why the damage to the peat bog at Loch Duich
on the Isle of Islay by the malt whisky distillers was such a
tragedy. The white-fronted geese which have overwintered
there for thousands of years simply will not change that pattern
and move to somewhere else. They are much more likely to
die out instead. If you create your shallow water, and your
marshy meadows on the flight path of a traditional migration
route, then you stand a good chance of attracting visitors.
Snipe, for instance, fly by night, and on moonlit evenings
the old poachers tempt them down to apparently waterlogged

fields, by pinning sheets of aluminium foil to the grass. These reflect the moonlight, look like puddles of water, and provide the hunters with birds oven-ready.

Many of our best traditional wintering grounds were on the mudflats and sea-washed turf of our river estuaries. Sadly, most of this great wetland heritage was swamped with industrial buildings during the last century, and is now covered by hundreds of acres of factories, warehouses and dockland paraphernalia. The rivers are still there, and now that the industries of Merseyside, Humberside, Tyneside and the rest are all in rapid decline, the waterways are beginning to clean themselves. Much of this nineteenth century development is deserted and derelict. It has outlived its usefulness, and with container-handling, direct rail links to the Continent, and the growth of air freight, it is unlikely that we will ever need all that estuarine industrial land again. Whether that is true or not, the fact remains that, for the time being at least, there is an enormous amount of flat, ugly coastal land lying idle, in locations which are the traditional wintering ground for internationally migrating wildlife. Isn't it time we adopted some of that land, even temporarily, and converted it to renewed coastal wetland habitat? Simple wind-pumps could divert river water on to the demolition flat-lands. We could quickly establish reed-beds and mud-flats, shingle beaches and shallow pools. We could even boost the invertebrate food supply by spreading slurry from our factory farms, or laying down layers of municipal compost over the concrete. The high security fences would provide the sanctuary the wildfowl need, and if the experiment was spread widely enough, we could create a mosaic of individual wetlands which would better anything the rest of Europe can offer. Should sites in fact be needed for new buildings, then this kind of habitat is easily undone, and one or two islands of industry in a 'natural' landscape setting might offer just the appeal which could reduce developer pressure in the countryside.

It would take very little temporarily to reclaim this precious estuary land for wildlife. The research has already been done at artificially created wetlands such as the RSPB reserve at Minsmere, on the Suffolk coast, and the Game Conservancy's project at Milton Keynes. Britain would be putting back something of great value to the world, and far more people in our ports and seaside towns would thrill to the sound of wild geese, flying in from the frozen north to their traditional wintering grounds in the safety of the city.

URBAN WOODLANDS

10

For thousands of years, from the end of the last Ice Age, up until the time when man began cutting and burning for agriculture, Britain was virtually covered by forest. Almost every village and town started life long ago as a clearing in the forest. There are still a few tiny fragments of that wild wood left, where for nearly 8000 years there has been a rich community of woodland wildlife. The vast majority of it has gone, however, and in recent years the rate of loss has speeded up. After a lull of several hundred years, we have suddenly started grubbing out, chopping down and destroying our last small relics in a greedy attempt to steal a little more land for wheat fields, housing estates, motorways, warehouses and reservoirs. It is always easy to argue that this is 'progress' and that modern Britain needs these things – but every compromise is really a loss when we're dealing with ancient woodland, and time and again the benefits promised by the destruction lobby never actually materialise.

When a woodland goes, we lose an irreplaceable part of our heritage. I recently helped fight to stop a road being built slap through the middle of a 45-acre relic of ancient oak woodland in north Worcestershire. The engineers, the planners and most of the local people seemed to feel that this route was best because it put the road out of sight. The woodland itself is wonderful. It is owned by the Methodist Church, and they use it as a 'retreat' for people from the city, and children in particular, to escape for a snatch of natural peace and quiet. Within the wood, the big old oaks overshadow a rich understorey of hazel and rowan, bramble and honeysuckle, and in spring when the sun is still able to filter down through the branches, the wood is carpeted in a pastel kaleidoscope of wildflowers. Bluebells are the stars, but there are sheets of white wood anemone, pockets of yellow archangel, shy little clusters of violets, banks of primroses, and around the edge, where the light is brightest, there are spectacular borders of pink campion and foxgloves. The animal life in this wood is remarkable, too. There are two extensive badger setts, both directly on the line of the proposed road, each at a point where the engineers designed a deep cutting. There are masses of birds, with the green and greater-spotted woodpeckers being perhaps the most exciting. They thrive thanks to the large number of mature oaks, the ample dead branches, occasional dying silver birch, and in the case of the green woodpecker, a nearby pasture sprinkled with anthills. Green woodpeckers just love eating ants. Butterflies such as the speckled wood, the brimstone and even the purple emperor are plentiful here, and there is the kind of rich and varied community of creepy-crawlies which you only find in the leaf-litter of really ancient woodlands. These wild animals and plants are the direct descendants of ancestors that lived here thousands of years ago. The badger setts, for instance, almost certainly have a history going back hundreds of years and there will have been badgers here 'forever'. How sad to think that we might be the generation that finally drives them out or kills them off. This district of north Worcestershire has already lost a square mile of woodland in the last ten years. That is a large area to lose forever in such a short time – a patch the size of a small town within the boundaries of just one district council.

That woodland, like every other, has a rish *human* history too. We are the latest in a long line of local people who have all shared it. Every generation up until the last war was able to live in caring harmony with their wood. They coppiced hazel stems to make wattle for buildings and fences and gates. They cropped the oaks, too. The beams in the local Saxon church and the Norman manor house were once oaks growing there. How can we possibly wipe out all of that history, just to hide a road?

Of course, the destruction lobby will immediately tell us, 'We've planted more trees in the past fifty years than ever before.' That is true. Whilst our lowland broad-leaved woods, with their oaks and hazels, primroses and bluebells, woodpeckers and nuthatches, have been cleared away, our wild, wet, windswept and less expensive uplands have been covered with new trees. These barren moorlands are not well suited to growing fine broad-leaved trees, and so we have imported tougher foreign species that can grow in the near-Arctic conditions, and produce a timber crop within

Everyone should have a local woodland to walk in, but we now have very little left.

Once-common woodland wildflowers such as the primrose have become rare and unfamiliar.

thirty or forty years. These 'wonder trees' are evergreen conifers. Their plantations blanket the hilltops in a dark 'unnatural' green. Being alien, their origin mainly North American, they support little or no insect life when growing in Britain, and will take thousands of years in residence before they build up a respectable population of the associated wildlife community typical of native species.

The conifers are planted closely together for maximum efficiency, so cutting out all light and leaving the forest floor barren, dry and lifeless. The best you can hope for in the way of wildlife is gloom-tolerant ferns and fungi, the occasional valiant wren, and winter flocks of small seed-eating birds in the treetops high above.

Despite all this upland coniferisation, we still import 90% of the timber we need, and so obviously there is pressure to grow more and more of our own. More new, broad-leaved, deciduous woodland in the lowlands would seem to make good sense. The publicly owned land is the obvious place to start, and you should be able to persuade the parks committee to launch a programme of new woodland development in public open spaces.

There is a good deal of private land which is suitable, too. Flat development sites with an expensive services infrastructure will probably be too highly valued for such a long-term green use. There is, however, perhaps 10% of all this development land which will never be built on. It is too steeply sloping, small scale or unstable for new buildings. Urban forestry here would improve the landscape greatly, and might even improve the chances of attracting commercial redevelopment to the remaining 90%. In the farming landscape, intensive food production is still the order of the day, though this is changing dramatically, and since farmers respond so readily to financial manipulation, it would take very little, I suspect, to promote a good deal of serious woodland planting and management on farms. So far as most of us are concerned, the obvious place where we would most like to see woodlands filled with wildlife, cared for as part of normal commercial management, is in our local neighbourhood. There is a huge amount of land in our towns, cities and villages, often ideally suited to growing trees, and much of it is standing idle, waiting for some positive new use. The answer, in many cases, could be community woodland. It's an idea that is already catching on in some towns, and there is no reason at all why yours shouldn't be the next neighbourhood to start its own woodland project. The Forestry Commission even offer very generous grants to pay for preparation, planting and the early years of establishment, and they should be happy for you to start with an area as small as half a football pitch.

Naturally, an increase of woodland in towns would mean more birdlife, more butterflies and, in time, more wildflowers, too. Urban woodland has much, much more to offer us, though, than wildlife habitat. In some of the larger German and Dutch cities, where urban forestry has been practised for decades, there is plenty of evidence to show how valuable woodland can be in other ways. Trees are very efficient pollution-filters. As the wind blows through a block of trees, the leaves trap the dust, and this washes to the ground in the next shower of rain. As a result the air downwind of your wood is cleaner. Leaves can remove a good deal of a town's chemical air pollution too, though of course there is a limit. If pollution gets too severe then the trees themselves will die. That is what seems to be at least a part of the problem with the forests of Sweden and West Germany, where acid rain is being blamed for the death of millions of trees. I must say, though, that an atmosphere which is polluted enough to kill a tree is certainly no place for people to live, and there is another reason for urban forestry. It could act as a useful indicator of the environmental quality we are all sharing.

Many of our towns and cities are very windy places. Tall buildings and large flat landscapes tend to encourage the breeze to speed up, and then be whipped into a frenzy of litter and dust – not at all comfortable! Urban woodlands offer valuable shelter, and in slowing down windspeed they would help insulate the buildings themselves, and so reduce the cost of heating in the winter and air-conditioning in the summer. That kind of hidden benefit would always be difficult to measure, but with modern scientific techniques it is possible to compare the energy costs of sheltered and unsheltered structures, and over the life of most buildings, the cost of the woodland would be repaid in energy savings.

A well-managed woodland could contribute to energy conservation in another, more direct way too. Firewood is a renewable energy resource. What that means is that, with care, we can keep using trees as a convenient way of storing up the sun's free energy, and our fuel will never run out. At the moment we in Britain depend almost entirely on the burning of fossil fuels, particularly coal and oil, for our heating, for generating electricity, and for running our transport. One day those sources of power will run out, but a carefully managed wood will keep on producing fuel forever. I am not suggesting we return to the 'Good King Wenceslas' era, with poor men gathering winter fuel from the local urban woodland, although in the miners' strike of 1984–5 there was a spectacular return to firewood-gathering in order to keep a good many families warm, and I know of quite a few poorer housing estates, where unemployment is well over 60% and firewood-gathering is gradually eating away at the local landscape. This kind of casual, often desperate cropping tends to destroy the resource itself. That is a large part of the problem of desertification in the Third World, where trees are cut down for firewood at a far more rapid rate than they are being replanted or are naturally recovering. The key to successful long-term urban forestry in Britain is to manage it carefully, and crop just as much each year as the forest can itself replace either through sucker re-growth or seedling germination. There is a considerable market in the countryside these days for logs to fuel wood-burning stoves and the open fires of cosy village pubs. But if log-burning returned on a grand scale to the towns it would create terrible air pollution problems, and in most cases, the log-burners would, in fact, be breaking the pollution laws.

There is, however, a very real non-polluting alternative use

HIGH CANOPY FOREST TREES

Oak	*Quercus robur* on deep rich lowland soils
Oak	*Quercus petraea* on poorer, bleaker sites
Beech	*Fagus sylvatica* on thin chalky soils
Ash	*Fraxinus excelsior* on richer limy soils
Hornbeam	*Carpinus betulus* on damp lowland soils
Alder	*Alnus glutinosa* on wet soil
White willow	*Salix alba* on waterlogged soils
Small-leaved lime	*Tilia cordata* on rich soil
Wild cherry *or* Gean	*Prunus avium* on rich soil

Avoid planting exotic woodland trees, particularly horse chestnut (*Aesculus hippocastaenum*); sweet chestnut (*Castanea sativa*); Norway maple (*Acer platanoides*); sycamore (*Acer pseudoplatanus*) and evergreen conifers. These species suppress most wildlife.

for woodland fuel crops. The Scandinavians have developed a range of burners which can take finely chopped wood, even when it is fresh and still green, and burn it very efficiently. The whole of the wood is burned and reburned to produce a great deal of heat. The only waste product is a tiny amount of fine grey ash. One or two of these furnaces are already in use in Britain – using woodland waste to heat the glasshouses in parks departments, for instance. In Belfast there is a plan to grow woodland on the windswept surface of completed refuse disposal tips, and to use the chopped wood to help in burning future domestic refuse. I see no reason why we could not grow timber on a grand scale in towns, simply to use in this way for heating schools, for instance, or even for fuelling district heating schemes for housing. The combination of woodland shelter and renewable energy would increase the efficiency of our wasteful urban lifestyle a great deal.

The most effective way of producing this kind of green woodchip energy-crop would be to plant fast-growing species which could be cut to the ground on a three-year cycle. This kind of 'coppice' is extremely productive. There are certain species of willow and poplar which can produce shoots over ten feet tall in the first year following cropping. They are not particularly valuable plantations for wildlife, however, so a mixture of short-cycle coppice areas and long-term more normal woodlands would be the best system to follow. Alder coppice and wild cherry would be a particularly useful mixed crop. The resulting woodland would be fast-growing, attractive to look at, valuable for wildlife, and the alder would even trap its own nitrogen and be self-fertilising.

By now you are probably asking what on earth I think all this has got to do with ordinary folk like us. Well, for a start, we would obviously all gain a great deal if there was more woodland in towns. Apart from the cleaner air, the gentler sheltered climate and the chance to save a few bob on fuel, there is plenty of scientific evidence to show that green leaves and woodland wildlife have a soothing, calming effect on people. Why else would the London parks fill up with office workers each lunchtime? Why else would our dream home be a cottage in the phantom leafy countryside? If we want urban woodland, then it is up to us to make it happen. We are the people who need to persuade politicians; to find

These lucky children now know that 'a wood' is much more than just 'a bunch of old trees'. The sounds and smells of a bluebell wood are quite unforgettable, yet this one is threatened by a bypass, and we have destroyed as much of this marvellous habitat in the past forty years as our ancestors cleared in the previous four hundred.

PIONEER TREES AND SHRUBS

OPEN GRAVELLY SOILS AND RUBBLE

Silver birch	*Betula pendula*
Goat willow *or* pussy willow	
	Salix capraea
Bramble *or* blackberry	
	Rubus fruticosus
Elder	*Sambucus nigra*
Sycamore*	*Acer pseudoplatanus*
False acacia*	*Robinia pseudoacacia*
Tree lupin*	*Lupinus arborea*
Bladder senna*	*Colutea arborescens*
Broom	*Cytisus scoparius*
Alder	*Alnus glutinosa*

* Not native. Use only as a last resort

GRASS AND VEGETATED SOIL

Oak	*Quercus robur* and
	Quercus petraea
Ash	*Fraxinus excelsior*
Bramble	*Rubus fruticosus*
Dog rose *or* briar	*Rosa canina*
Blackthorn *or* sloe	*Prunus spinosa*
Gorse	*Ulex europaea*
Hawthorn	*Crataegus monogyna*
	or *C. oxycantha*

the suitable land; to make sure the right kinds of trees and shrubs are planted correctly, and to take a hand in caring for the woodland. At present, those community woodlands that do exist are managed by volunteers in their spare time. That is marvellous, and produces all kinds of positive spin-offs, but in the long term, when we have tens of thousands of acres of thriving urban woodland, we will have a new industry on our hands which, because it is productive as well as beautiful, can provide enjoyable paid employment for a great many people who live in towns.

You will remember I talked about re-vitalising the barren fragments of relict woodland in our city parks. Well, the multi-layered structure of those renewed woods is the kind of pattern we should be aiming for with our new plantations, but in this case we are starting pretty well from scratch.

Most of us live in lowland Britain. That is where our towns and cities were built. Because the natural vegetation is broad-leaved woodland, it really is relatively easy to grow new woods. In fact, in every patch of bare, treeless open space there is a new wood, desperate to burst into life. It is the simple, regular business of mowing and trampling that prevents this from happening. Have a think about your own neighbourhood. Wherever a piece of green space has been left for more than five or six years, woodland will have started to develop. On the old abandoned railway sidings, on the redundant sand-pit or the brick-rubble of the demolition site you will have sycamore, silver birch, ash and perhaps the odd buddleia bush and elderberry. These are the pioneer tree species which are able to move in and thrive on little or no soil.

If your emergent woodland is growing in an area that was once grass – say a road embankment or a farmer's abandoned field, then the tree and shrub community will be different. Here the pioneers are more likely to be hawthorn, wild rose, oak and bramble. The easiest way to begin developing urban woodland is simply to encourage this process, which is called natural succession, to take place wherever it can. If there is a corner of the school playing field that is not used for football or hockey, keep the mowing machine out, let the grass grow, and you will very quickly find shrubby, woody pioneers moving in. It makes a marvellous school study project, to map the patch each year and see just how the vegetation develops. There are huge areas of grassland which could be encouraged to develop as new woodland. Some of it may be of more value to us as flowering grassland, cut just a couple of times a year to keep out the woody pioneers, but if we were to do no more than encourage woodland to colonise all the grassy slopes which are actually very difficult to mow, that would add up to an enormous acreage of urban land, and in a decade or two we really would have ribbons of woodland to clean the air along our motorways and railways, to shelter the players on all those terraced sports fields, and green up the view in the ugliest of our towns and cities.

You can give this kind of 'grassland-to-woodland' process a bit of a boost, too. Left to their own devices it will be quite a while before the hawthorn and the rose-hip seeds start to arrive. They are delivered by fruit-eating birds such as blackbirds, thrushes and starlings. Colonisation happens fastest in those edge-of-town pastures, chopped by a new road or an industrial estate, but still edged by hedgerow. The hedge is full of just the kinds of trees and shrubs that can colonise uncropped grassland. There is a marvellous example that I pass every day on my drive through Birmingham. Several fields were left redundant after a new 'expressway' was built. These old pastures have been abandoned now for ten years or more. The field hedgerows have grown up to form narrow strips of tall vegetation, and on either side there is now a dense colony of pioneers. The trees and shrubs have reached sixteen feet already, and the grassland habitat is well on the way to being a wood.

Your chosen patch of green may not be so fortunate. It could be quite a long time before thorn scrub is sufficiently well established to persuade jays to carry in acorns from distant oak trees and plant them for you. Fortunately it is the simplest thing in the world quietly, even secretly, to play the role of surrogate jay or blackbird. Oaks are easiest to introduce because acorns are so convenient to handle and they do grow well in grassland. Just collect some freshly ripened nuts, choosing that moment when they first fall from the trees and are still green. Take them to your grassy bank, kick a notch in the turf with your heel, or use a trowel if you prefer, and then simply push an acorn an inch or so down through the turf into the soil below. Press it in with your toe, and, hey presto, you've launched another oak tree! You can't really do quite the same thing with smaller seed. Firstly it is difficult to handle, and secondly, the process by which the blackbird digests the soft flesh of the fruit actually prepares the indigestible seed in some way so that afterwards it germinates

COUNTRY HEDGEROW SHRUBS

Also ideal for gardens and school boundaries

Hawthorn	*Crataegus monogyna*
Buckthorn	*Prunus spinosa*
Field maple	*Acer campestre*
Guelder rose	*Viburnum opulus*
Dog rose	*Rosa canina*
Wild privet	*Ligustrum vulgaris*
Holly	*Ilex aquifolium*
Oak	*Quercus robur*

UNDER-STOREY WOODLAND SHRUBS

for including in mixed planting for new woods, or planting under the old trees of relic woodland in 'green desert' parks

Hazel	*Corylus avellana*
Hawthorn	*Crataegus monogyna*
Bird Cherry	*Prunus padus*
Holly	*Ilex aquifolium*
Wild privet	*Ligustrum vulgaris*
Rowan	*Sorbus aucuparia*
Elder	*Sambucus nigra*
Dog rose	*Rosa canina*
Box	*Buxus sempervirens*
Yew	*Taxus baccata*

NB Don't plant bramble. It will arrive on its own soon enough.

Old industrial scars such as this quarry have become heavily wooded quite naturally, simply by being left to nature. With a little encouragement we could afforest the modern scars much more rapidly.

much more readily.

So far I've never met anyone who has managed to train blackbirds to eat hawthorn berries in one place, and then fly on bombing missions over selected woodland development sites. Unless you are particularly gifted in this respect – a family background in the circus perhaps – you really need to introduce your hawthorn, wild rose and bramble as rooted seedlings, preferably when they are four or five inches tall. It is possible to buy such seedlings very cheaply from a nursery, but it is quite nice to have a go at growing your own. If you can find a bush of your chosen grassland pioneer species which overhangs a paved area, then you may actually be able to sweep up seeds which have passed through the guts of roosting birds, but if that really does strike you as an impossible task, don't despair. Collect some of the fresh berries and fruits in the autumn, crush them or even put them briefly into a liquidiser to squeeze out the seeds, and then wash the pulp over and over again. This seems to remove some of the chemicals which prevent germination. A quick rinse with vinegar and some other weak acid seems to help even more.

Spread the seed on the surface of a shallow plant pot or seed tray filled with gritty compost; sprinkle a little sand over the top, just enough to cover the seed, then place outside, in the coldest, frostiest corner you can find. Once the spring arrives, move your 'nursery' to a warmer corner, water it lightly, and some of the seed will germinate. As soon as you have four leaves on a seedling, carefully 'prick' it out and plant it into a pot of its own, or into a corner of the garden. Leave it to grow through that first summer. Don't throw your pot of seed away either. You will almost certainly find that many of the seeds don't germinate until the second spring.

There is no need to plant up your whole grassy bank with seedlings. Plant them in groups, with each seedling perhaps a yard or so from the next, and don't mix the bramble seedlings with anything else. They grow more quickly and will swamp slower species.

These thorny pioneers will grow rapidly once they get started, and within as little as three years you will find that some of them are flowering, producing fruit and beginning to colonise the rest of the area all on their own.

There is of course a limit to the amount of colonisable grassland you are likely to have in your neighbourhood. The wasted land resource we seem to have an endless supply of is the ugly, blighted demolition land of redundant industry, the abandoned quarries and railway land. Here there is often a problem of ownership and access. We have over 10,000 acres of this kind of ugly dereliction in the Black Country alone. Some of it is in huge hundred-acre lumps where a steelworks has gone. The problem is that, for the most part, the owners of this desolate landscape refuse to believe that their site will not be needed for future industrial buildings. The land itself has a theoretical value, fixed by accountants, which effectively sterilises it and prevents any kind of long-term alternative use. I have to admit that it will be a long time before the big, flat, easily accessible, stable sites are given over to greening. Indeed there is still a huge amount of public money being poured into creating even more of these 'hope-value' deserts. If you have done your habitat network survey properly, you will have noticed that many of these demolition sites are an inconvenient shape for development, with tight triangles of land in one corner for instance, or long, narrow, inconvenient strips of land. In all the effort to create developable flat plateaux, inevitably there are steep banks produced around the edges, and there is often land which has been parcelled together with a buildable site, but which is not itself stable enough for building. Now, picture all of those spare pockets and banks covered by woodland. You can see how much that would improve the wildlife network – patching up the gaps between railway cutting and canal

Hawthorn, or May blossom, is one of our most beautiful native trees, and certainly one of the very best for wildlife. It is quick to colonise abandoned grassland. Birds eat the haws in autumn, and so transport the seed to new sites where scrub woodland soon begins to appear.

We have no shortage of land suitable for urban forestry. Even if developers continue to build on flat sites like this, there are thousands of acres of sloping or unstable ground where trees could grow.

corridor, for instance. Imagine what a difference all that securely
protected woodland would make to the number of songbirds,
hedgehogs and other wild creatures in our towns. There is
no reason why we can't look forward to that scale of urban
forestry, without taking away any of the genuinely reusable
building land. Perhaps most exciting of all, the belts of
woodland which would then surround, enclose and shelter
the development sites might make them more attractive to
developers. It would make working in the industrial
landscape more acceptable to the high-fliers of the modern
'science-park' and might eventually reduce the pressure to
build on virgin sites in the green fields on the edge of town.

Redundant heavy industry is not the only source of this
kind of barren, rubble-strewn demolition land. Cleared
housing, mining spoil, worked out gravel pits, military camps
and abandoned airfields all offer similar potential.

If you have land like this in your neighbourhood, and you
want to have a go, then first of all you will obviously have to
seek the co-operation of the landowner. That is often more
difficult than you might think, but in chapter twelve I will
be giving you a few clues about where to begin your detective
work. Imagine for the time being that you have permission,
your sloping pile of earth and rubble is available, and you have
gathered together a merry band of urban foresters to help
you out. Please don't think that you need to plant any of those
big, expensive standard trees that parks departments and
highway engineers seem to go in for. They are a disastrous
waste of money. In Britain we spend about a hundred million
pounds annually on ornamental planting, and precious little
of it survives its first five years, let alone growing into
anything which resembles a wood – remember 'Plant a tree
in '73'? Where are they now? The truth is that nearly all of
them died within a year or two of planting. A big tree grown
in the shelter of a nursery simply can't cope with the tough,
exposed conditions we are dealing with. Small trees are a
fraction of the cost, and they survive transplanting so much
better. Buy plants from a reliable nursery, and aim to put one
tree or shrub into each square yard of ground. Do measure
the area on the ground. If you try and work out the number
of plants you need for a steep bank, simply by measuring
the area on a paper plan, you get a distorted picture and will
finish up very short of material.

Choose trees and shrubs which grow naturally in the kind
of material you are dealing with. If it is mainly rubble and

WOODLAND FLOOR WILDFLOWERS

Mostly spring flowering,
and over by the time the
leaf canopy closes above.
Plant them along
hedgerows, too

Bluebell	*Endymion non-scriptus*
Wood spurge	*Euphorbia amygdaloides*
Wood anemone	*Anemone nemorosa*
Lily of the valley	*Convallaria majalis*
Red campion	*Silene dioica*
Yellow archangel	
	Lamiastrum galeobdolon
Dog violet	*Viola riviniana*
Primrose	*Primula vulgaris*
Woodruff	*Galium odoratum*
Wood avens *or* herb bennet	
	Geum urbanum
Lesser celandine	*Ranunculus ficaria*
Snowdrop	*Galanthus nivalis*
Ramsons	*Allium ursinum*
Foxglove	*Digitalis purpurea*
Wild daffodil	
	Narcissus pseudo-narcissus
Wild strawberry	*Fragaria vesca*
Wood sorrel	*Oxalis acetosella*

OPPOSITE: *1. Plant straight into
rubble and prune all side shoots
back to buds. 2. Drench the roots
with lots of water as soon as the
tree is planted. 3. 'Mulch' with a
sheet of black polythene, thick
cardboard or old carpet to smother
weed competition and keep the
ground moist.*

stone without any soil, then you'll be surprised to hear that
this is very good news. Don't be tempted to spread any soil
on top. If you do, all that will happen is that a jungle of weeds
will spring up, and they will kill your preferred trees and
shrubs by out-competing them for moisture. The trees and
shrubs to choose for rubble are silver birch, ash, English alder,
goat willow, broom and gorse. None of these plants needs
rich soil to grow in, but they do need moisture, so I always
make sure I plant in the dormant season, when the plants
are without leaves, and then find some way of drenching the
root-zone with water at the beginning of the first growing
season. There are a number of additional things you can do,
too, to increase the chances of survival and establishment.
First of all, make sure your tree and shrub roots never dry
out, even for a few minutes. An experiment a friend of mine
carried out with seedling silver birch showed that if the roots
were exposed to the air, even for as little as half an hour,
that was enough to kill the plants, no matter how well they
were then planted and cared for. I dip the roots of my plants
in a special kind of 'gunge' made from seaweed. It is something
called an alginate, and is now available in the better garden
centres, and it does seem to help new roots form, and take up
more moisture. It smells of the seaside, too, and if you are
involving children in the planting, you'll find they love the
smell and the messiness of the gunge.

After planting, always prune off some of the side shoots.
With shrubs such as goat willow and hawthorn I chop the
whole plant down to a few inches. This helps reduce leaf-area
at the start of the first season, compensates for any roots
which the plant has lost in transplanting, and I am convinced
it helps them establish more quickly.

Finally, there is much to be gained by keeping each plant
completely clear of weeds. Obviously you don't want to start
using weedkillers if your main aim is conservation, so I
recommend you provide each new plant with a mulching
'collar'. Black polythene, old carpet or even thick cardboard
will do the job. You need a piece of material, about a yard
square, with a slit from one edge to the centre. When this is
laid over the 'soil' and weighted down with stones, it stops
the weeds growing, and keeps the moisture high up amongst
the plant's developing roots. Cardboard and carpet both rot
away in two or three years, when their job is done, but
polythene does have to be removed by hand.

In many old industrial areas, the first stage of colonisation

and woodland development is well advanced. We have a wonderful quarry near where I live which has sixty years of birch and thorn growth in it, and there are many examples of old ballast and ash-covered railway sidings which became redundant with the Beeching cuts in the 1950s, and have since developed a dense cover of pioneers. Even the grassy motorway verges that were all mown neatly until the late 1960s have now been abandoned long enough for some quite respectable hawthorn scrub to develop. What all of these pioneer communities lack – your own new planting included – is the carpet of wildflowers, the old rotting logs and the so-called 'climax tree species' that together make up true woodland. Once your scrub has formed a dense cover, you should think about introducing more seedling trees of species such as wild gean or cherry, whitebeam, oak, beech and lime. With the shelter provided by your 'front line', these less resilient forest species will thrive, and eventually they will grow up tall enough to overshadow the sun-loving pioneers. Within about ten years you can begin thinning out some of the early pioneers, and so taking off your first crops. When shredded, these thin stems of birch, willow, etc are suitable for burning, but I think this first thinning is best either chopped into four-inch pieces and returned to the woodland floor as a mulch, or tied in loose bundles and stacked in quiet corners of the landscape to provide more nesting sites for wrens, blackbirds and robins.

If you thin a different patch each year, to let more sunlight in, you will create more diversity of habitat. Wildflowers such as foxglove and red campion will thrive if planted into the glades, and you will also find that the woodland butterflies tend to be more common in the dappled shade of the thinned areas.

As soon as the first stage of woodland vegetation is established, there will be a population explosion amongst the voles, woodmice and other small mammals. This will attract predators such as the stoat, weasel and fox. As this leaf-litter builds up, and dead logs begin to rot down, you can expect to see a whole new complex community of woodland insects, fungi and other lowly species begin to appear.

It will take ten to fifteen years before your new woodland closes over your head and begins to sound and smell like a real wood, but long before that it will be slowing down the wind, filtering the air and greatly improving the wild side of town, for wildlife and, of course, for people too.

This 'woodland' was planted less than fifteen years ago. Already it is casting dappled shade and is full of wildflowers and songbirds.

MINI-HABITATS AT GARDEN SCALE

11

I t is exciting to talk of wetlands for migratory geese, forests to heat our towerblocks, and herds of deer roaming the grassland of the city park. Believe me, they will all happen if you want them to and if you are prepared to get down to the boring business of writing letters, applying for grants and attending meetings before you actually get to see any results on the ground. In the meantime, there is a lot you can do on a smaller scale to create a real mini-habitat in your own back yard.

You can begin in a very modest way. There is no need to abandon your rose-beds and vegetable patch. In fact you need a reasonable number of 'normal' garden features in order to make the best service station possible. Try thinking of your garden as a woodland glade. Remember that most of our small garden birds and mammals are woodland refugees, and certainly some of our prettiest wildflowers originate in woodland habitat too. The main thing which turns a group of trees from a plantation into a woodland is the increasing amount of decay. The same goes for rich-habitat gardens. You should stop burning things, and find ways of letting garden-waste rot down graciously. Gardeners are preoccupied with tidying up, and that is the kiss of death to garden wildlife. Remember all those pleas from *Gardeners' Question Time* to burn the dead seed-heads, for fear of harbouring pests and diseases? Well, those pests and diseases are garden wildlife, and in our efforts to destroy them we have been killing an awful lot of useful and interesting plants and animals at the same time.

Step one must be to construct a compost heap. In fact construct two compost heaps. Then you can be building up the second whilst the first one gently decomposes. Choose a secluded corner of the garden. Good compost probably won't smell, but it can attract flies whilst the material is fresh, and in any case a compost heap isn't particularly pretty. The main requirement for good compost is plenty of air, contact

Decay is the secret of a successful rich habitat garden. If you must sweep up the leaves, please leave them in a secret corner where they can rot down.

with the soil, and protection from torrential rain. There are some excellent composting bins available, made from plastic and very respectable-looking. They are expensive, however, and not terribly easy for larger animals to make use of. The simplest thing is to build home-made bins using timber corner-stakes and a series of horizontal planks with wide gaps between them. Make two open-fronted, open-topped boxes measuring about three feet in each dimension. Tack some galvanised chicken wire to the inside of each bin, to keep the composting material in, and then begin building up the vegetable matter. The aim is to produce a concentrated heap of plant material, and rely upon the worms, slugs and particularly the microscopic creatures that decompose things, to turn all your weeds, cabbage leaves, egg shells etc., into lovely, dark, crumbly compost, full of nutrients and just right for putting back into the soil.

Once the heap of kitchen and garden waste reaches the top of bin one, lift it over in forkfuls to the second bin, and build it up in six-inch layers, treading each one down firmly, sprinkling it with a little nitrogen-rich fertiliser, old compost or one of the organic compost boosters if you want swift results, and then eventually giving the completed heap a thorough soaking, and topping off with a lump of old carpet or a perforated sheet of black polythene. This covering keeps in the warmth and stops the compost becoming too soggy in heavy rain. As the decomposition squad gets underway, the temperature of your heap should rise. If not, then it is probably not getting enough air, and you might try poking a few holes into it with a fork or an iron bar. Include some green grass-clippings in one or two of the layers too. These build up a higher temperature than coarser material. Once the temperature does build up, then most material should be fully composted within six months, though tougher things like cabbage stalks, holly leaves and rose prunings take much longer, and are probably best left out altogether, or concentrated at the base of the heap to improve air circulation. For the very best results, it really does pay to put everything through a shredder. This means you can include the tougher material, but mechanical shredders are expensive and by no means essential.

With so many wriggly little creatures living in one place, it is hardly surprising that the larger predators soon start to call, and a good compost heap can expect to pull in toads, hedgehogs, robins, blackbirds, thrushes and shrews on a regular basis. The warmth is a great attraction too, and if you are lucky enough to have grass-snakes or slow worms in your neighbourhood, they could well choose the warm comfort of your compost heap in which to breed.

All your dry dead seed-heads and prunings can be used for a different kind of mini-habitat. Don't mix them with your compost and please don't burn them either. Bundle them together instead and cram them into a quiet corner where they can shelter more wildlife. You will be astonished by the number of ladybirds, for instance, that will gather together in the crevices of a dead seed-head and so survive the winter. When spring returns they will be there on the spot, ready to leap off and start mopping up the first of your greenfly. Burn the seed-heads, and you will be destroying a lot of your garden's natural pesticide squad. We have raspberries in our garden, and I always make a point of cutting the old canes into manageable lengths, tying them in bundles and wedging them under the hedge. You can do the same with the clearings from the herbaceous border, too.

A rotting log is as good as a miniature nature reserve in its own right. If you have the chance, do create a log-pile habitat in your garden. Again, choose a secluded spot if you can, and just pile the logs loosely. If you are worried about spreading disease, particularly honey fungus, put the timber on a hard surface, or a sheet of polythene, to prevent direct contact with the soil, and don't pile your rotting logs against a fence or a wooden shed – it might join in. Even a small pile of logs will quickly provide a home for various wood-boring creatures, and some of them really are spectacular. The logs in my decay corner house a whole variety of woodwasps, for instance, and there are large tunnels, with sawdust-like 'frass' around the entrance, where various beetle larvae are hard at work each summer. The damp space beneath the logs is a favourite hibernation and sheltering place for many creatures. The rusty-coloured centipede and shiny black and silver millipede are always there, along with huge and handsome leopard slugs. Most exciting of all are the hibernating newts, and the baby frogs and toads that hide here in the first autumn after they leave the pond habitat which supports them through their tadpole phase.

One of the best ways of keeping down weeds in the garden is by covering the surface of shrub beds and flower borders with a mulch of some kind. This is just a thin layer of weed-free material, perhaps two or three inches thick, which allows air and water through to the soil, but doesn't let in the light that might trigger off weed-seed germination. You can use the compost you have made, of course. The high temperature of the heap should have killed off the weed seeds, though to be absolutely sure, it is best to add weeds to your compost only at the stage before they flower. Alternatively, you can now buy various bark and wood-chip mulches, either in pre-packed bags, or in larger lorry-loads. I think this is a great way to boost the garden habitat. It makes positive use of an otherwise wasted product. It helps to make woodland management economic. It looks good, reduces the amount of weeding you have to do, and the wildlife thrives on it. You only need to see how enthusiastically the blackbirds scratch around in amongst the chopped bark mulch, to know that it quickly builds up a rich community of mini-beasts. Mix in an inch or two of autumn leaves and you have a mini-habitat very similar to that of the woodland floor where all the blackbirds of long ago found their food.

Once decay has been accepted as a part of your everyday life, the next ingredient to think about is 'cover'. The majority of wild creatures are shy and secretive. Most gardens are short of hiding places. Forget about freshly hoed soil, spaces between the plants, and newly painted fences. Cover every possible surface with a dense canopy of plants. By all means keep your rose-bed, but underplant it with groundcover plants, or at least sow flowering annuals for the summer. Let the plants in your flower borders and shrubberies grow together until their leaves are intermingled and no sunlight can pass through to the soil below. This makes very good gardening sense, since it suppresses the weeds, but it also provides safe cover for hedgehogs, dunnocks, woodmice, beetles and a whole host of other garden wildlife. Many of our most interesting mammals are nocturnal – they feed by night and rest by day. They need safe places to hide until darkness falls, so the combination of leaf- and log-piles, with a dense canopy of trees, shrubs and groundcover plants is just what they need.

This dense 'undergrowth' is important for nesting and roosting birds, too. They need safe sites, out of the view of any predators. Some species such as the robin and the wren will nest close to the ground, but it isn't really very safe with so many marauding moggies around, so you need to create a little high-rise nesting habitat. If you have any walls or fences, cover them with climbers. Ivy is particularly useful because it

A spider-full garden is a healthy wildlife habitat. All those beautiful webs are a sure sign that your mini-meadow has plenty of little mini-beasts living in it, ready to be eaten.

is evergreen, its flowers and fruit are valuable on the service station menu, and if you can provide the odd ledge or shallow nesting tray behind the foliage, then blackbirds, robins, spotted flycatchers, wrens and hedge sparrows could all show an interest. If you don't have a fence or wall, then grow a hedge. This is a great way of providing nesting habitat, and if you plant a mixture of native shrubs and trees, you can support a huge range of insect species, too. Even in a small garden it is possible to grow a tapestry hedge of hawthorn, holly, wild privet, field maple, guelder rose, oak, beech, hornbeam and yew. Keep it tightly clipped and there will be insects galore, and dunnocks, greenfinches, thrushes and blackbirds queuing up to build nests.

You need to provide cover of a non-vegetable kind too. Try to think of yourself as a little furry animal, looking for somewhere to live. Now start to create the kind of habitat features you might be searching for. Piles of logs are good, and so are loose heaps of rocks. Try building a heap of stone, logs and soil, and then plant it with rockery plants or the kinds of wildflowers such as herb robert, navel-wort and stonecrop which naturally colonise stone walls. Pretty soon there will be bumblebees nesting there, and mice, and possibly a pair of wrens. I have built brick walls in our garden too, and designed them in such a way that I could leave holes in

Untidiness is in the eye of the beholder. What could be more charming than this flight of garden steps, colourfully colonised with ferns and wildflowers?

the centre of pillars, with a narrow entrance passage for inquisitive visitors. These are just like the natural cracks in trees and rocks where bluetits, great tits and wrens nest.

Even smaller holes than this are useful, and I have drilled a whole collection of 'tunnels' into the mortar of my brick walls. Here solitary bees nest, and to trap their prey, specialist spiders build funnels in the tunnels. You might like to try drilling holes in fence posts too. In no time at all you will see small black wood wasps flying in and out, depositing eggs in the wood itself, or in the larvae or eggs of other host insects. If you don't fancy the idea of your fence posts being chewed to bits, drive a few special stakes, or fix a few planks to the wall, for the exclusive use of the wildlife. Wherever you look, even in the tiniest garden, there is scope for improving habitat. If you have paving to lay, place the slabs on sand or soil instead of concrete. Ants will find the habitat and move in. Leave gaps between the paving slabs. A whole host of mosses and seeding wildflowers will find their way there and take up residence. We recently put up a new garden shed. Normally I would have set it on a base of solid concrete, but this time I built a framework of railway sleepers, with a gap in two of the sides, and the floor of the shed now sits over a snug, dry space about eighteen inches deep and a couple of square yards in area. All being well our local vixen will find this readymade earth, and choose it as the ideal place to give birth to some future litter of fox cubs.

There are over one million acres of garden in Britain, and at least half of that area is probably covered with lawn. Most of us are unlikely to attract skylarks to our modest 'pocket handkerchief', but it is well worth creating a mini-meadow habitat – however small. Make sure you keep some of your lawn close-mown, so that everyone knows you haven't simply abandoned the garden. Then let the rest of the lawn remain uncut, at least until June. You may be surprised to find a whole range of wildflowers growing which you never knew were there. In my case, milkmaids popped up and flowered, and so did yarrow and lesser stitchwort. There are plenty of specialist nurseries around these days which will sell you seed or pot grown plants, and even a tiny meadow can be rapidly turned into a tapestry of different colours and textures. On no account should you ever steal plants from the wild.

When it comes to mowing, you may well have a problem. The normal cylinder mower and rotary simply won't manage grass a foot tall. You will find it is much easier if you attempt your harvest when the grass is really dry, but even so it is difficult. For a tiny area, it is not too fanciful to make your hay with garden shears. What I do, however, is to hire a machine called a strimmer from my local garden centre for one day each year, and tackle the problem that way. The strimmer has a plastic blade, or a wire, which whizzes round at great speed, and once you get the hang of it, it is possible to produce a result which is as good as the cut the old scythes used to make. If you are really keen, of course, you can use a proper scythe, but that is pretty hard work. Once the hay is cut, and the seed of resident wildflowers has been shaken out by vigorous tossing, the crop must be removed. You can add it to the compost heap, dig it into the runner bean trench, or give it away to the local guinea pig stud, but whatever happens, you must rake it off the meadow area.

Our mini-meadow is only about five yards square, but even so, we have been delighted with the range of meadow wildlife it has attracted. I was astonished to hear grasshoppers fidgeting away in the second summer, and both meadow brown and common blue butterflies breed there each year. Bullfinches feed on the dandelion and cat's ear seed in late summer, and there are always spiders setting out their deadly webs amongst the grass stems. Peer down into the jungle, and the meadow is alive with strange creatures – ground beetles and ladybirds, harvestmen and money spiders, craneflies and dozens of other weird little mini-beasts I can't even begin to name. Again, this wealth of invertebrate life brings in the predators. Hedgehogs snuffle through the long grass on summer nights, dragonflies hunt over the surface, banking left or right to snap up smaller flying insects. Bats feed there on every balmy evening, and on more than one occasion, I have seen a kestrel hurl itself down into the long grass, intent on killing some poor unfortunate resident of my mini-meadow.

Those predatory dragonflies that spend the summer quartering the meadow must have a pool of unpolluted water in which to lay their eggs. A pond is certainly the most exciting addition you could ever wish to make to your rich habitat garden, and these days it is technically very simple. There is no escaping the need to dig a hole, I'm afraid, and this really must be at least eighteen inches deep in the centre. Choose a spot which is on level ground if you can, and well away from overhanging trees. There are several different ways of keeping the water in, but the most important thing from the

LARVAL FOOD PLANTS

for the caterpillars of town-dwelling butterflies

GRASSES

Couch (*Agropyron repens*) and Cocksfoot, particularly in dappled shade, for the speckled wood, ringlet and gatekeeper.

Annual meadow grass (*Poa annua*) for the wall brown and meadow brown.

Goat's tail grass, Soft creeping grass and Hop grass for the small skipper.

BROAD-LEAVED PLANTS

Stinging nettles (*Urtica dioica*) for the red admiral, small tortoiseshell, peacock, comma and painted lady.

Black medick (*Medicago lupulina*) or birdsfoot trefoil (*Lotus corniculatus*) for the common blue, green hairstreak and clouded yellow.

Ivy and holly flowers for alternate generations of the holly blue.

Sheep's sorrel (*Rumex acetosella*) or dock (*Rumex obtusifolius*) for the small copper.

Hedge mustard (*Sisymbrium officinale*) for the large white, small white, green-veined white and orange-tip.

Broom (*Cytisus scoparius*) for the green hairstreak.

Lady's smock (*Cardamine pratensis*) for the orange-tip and green-veined white.

Sweet rocket (*Hesperis matronalis*) and honesty (*Lunaria biennis*) for the orange-tip.

Nasturtium (*Tropaeolum majus*) for the large white.

Buckthorn (*Rhamnus catharticus*) for the brimstone.

Hop (*Humulus lupulus*) for the comma.

Moths are mostly just as specific in their food plant requirements as the butterfly larvae. A good many feed on meadow grasses, and goat willow (*Salix capraea*) is particularly useful.

wildlife habitat point of view, is that the pond must have shallow edges, and soil in the bottom for plants to grow in. If you decide to use a pre-formed fibreglass liner, you will find that these all have steep, slippery sides, and you actually have to start filling them in with rubble and subsoil if the wildlife is ever going to manage to climb safely in and out. Concrete tends to crack after a year or two, it is very hard work to build, and the chemicals in the cement mean you need to let the pond mature before introducing any plants or animals. I think the easiest and most effective method of lining a garden pond, is to use a sheet of flexible waterproof liner. Dig the hole like a very shallow-sided saucer, make sure that there are no sharp stones or fragments of glass in the bottom, and then stretch your liner over the hole, and cover it first with a four inch layer of subsoil, to protect the sheet and grow the plants. Once the soil is in, gently fill the pool with water, making sure you don't stir up the mud in the process. Tuck the edges of the liner under the surrounding turf, and expect to keep topping up the water for the first few days as it soaks up into the surrounding soil. This technique is suitable for all the different sheet liners, but if you can possibly afford it, do use the more expensive butyl sheeting. It is much tougher than the plastic. It stretches and it lasts much longer. For really first-class results, it is a good idea

This 'natural pond' won me a silver medal at the 1985 Chelsea Flower Show. The secret of success is to make the edges very gently sloping. Flag irises and other marginal plants will then disguise the edges and improve the habitat.

to dig a soak-away, add an overflow, and to collect rainwater from the nearby roof-gutters, instead of using tap water – but you will get marvellous results without bothering with any of these refinements.

Plant up your pond as soon as growth starts, in early spring, anchoring oxygenators firmly to the mud in the bottom, and providing a fringe of emergent marginal plants around the edge, and give this aquatic vegetation a whole year in which to establish before you bother to introduce animal life. Many of the flying invertebrates such as diving beetles, water boatmen and dragonflies will find a new pond on their own anyway, and if frogspawn or fish are introduced too soon, the plants won't stand a chance.

The combination of tap water and soil generally leads to a surplus of nutrients in the first year, and more often than not this produces an algal bloom of blanket weed. Don't, whatever you do, drain the pond and start again. That simply sends you back to square one. Just take a little trouble over raking out the green slime, pile it on the edge for a day or so, to let the wriggly things struggle back home, and then cart the blanket weed off to the compost heap. Unless you are very unlucky indeed, there will be little trouble with algae from the second summer onwards, since the bigger plants will be taking up the fertility.

The one kind of pond animal you really do need to make sure you have is the pond snail. This acts like a miniature vacuum cleaner, sucking up vegetable waste, and keeping the water crystal clear. Usually snails will arrive naturally as jelly-like clusters of eggs on the stems of the plants you introduce.

If your pond is big enough – and the general rule with ponds certainly is 'the bigger the better' – then try creating a marsh habitat at one end. I did this by separating off a shallow shelf in the pond, using elm log stepping stones, and filling in that shelf with subsoil. This stays permanently waterlogged, and provides the perfect habitat for a range of very beautiful marsh plants such as ragged robin, purple loosestrife and meadowsweet.

As genuine mini-habitats go, the garden pond really is magnificently successful. In the first week of March each year, dozens of frogs return, as if by magic, to mate in the icy shallows and lay their great blobs of spawn. Toads and newts soon follow, and even the rare and internationally protected great-crested newt breeds regularly in our three-year-old pond. Four species of dragonfly breed there too, and the

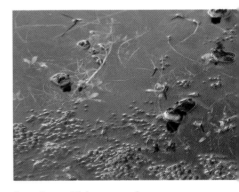

Introduce a blob or two of frogspawn to a new pond, and you will quickly establish a brand new breeding colony – but don't expect tadpoles to compete with goldfish.

NATIVE MARSH PLANTS

for growing in
waterlogged soil

Marsh marigold	*Caltha palustris*
Great hairy willowherb	
	Epilobium hirsutum
Flag iris	*Iris pseudacorus*
Ragged robin	*Lychnis flos-cuculi*
Purple loosestrife	*Lythrum salicaria*
Greater spearwort	
	Ranunculus lingua
Meadow sweet	*Filipendula ulmaria*
Hemp agrimony	
	Eupatorium cannabinum
Bugle	*Ajuga reptans*
Lesser celandine	*Ranunculus ficaria*

dragonfly larvae spend two or three years underwater, menacing the tadpole population before emerging to transform themselves into beautiful flying adults. Great diving beetles and their larvae hunt the tadpoles, too, and are as efficient as piranha fish at ripping the flesh from any poor injured animal that comes their way. I once watched eleven of these shining devils tear a dead frog to pieces in minutes.

Very few of the animals that live in the various mini-habitats of the wildlife garden are exclusive to one place. The pond snails are stuck in their pond, of course, and some of the slugs and snails rarely, if ever, leave the woodland edge, but most species move from habitat to habitat, and indeed many can only survive if they have variety. There are two particularly spectacular species of dragonfly which depend on the pond in our garden for breeding. The hawker is a long distance hunter, which hangs motionless for hours amongst the leaves and twigs of the hedgerow habitat, and quarters the woodland edge and the meadow hunting for its prey. It will move far and wide and I have even seen the occasional brave specimen dodging about amongst the cars and buses in the High Street. When its ugly, vicious, tadpole-eating larva leaves the water, it climbs up the leaves of marginal aquatic plants such as flag iris, flowering rush or spearwort, and then bursts from its shell and stretches out its wings to dry. By contrast, the broad-bodied darter is rather like an insect version of the spotted fly-catcher. It spends week after week hunting around our pond, with the powder blue male clearly establishing territory and returning time after time to its regular perch on a flowerhead or a leaf stem. When this species first emerges from the water, the larva crawls up the bank, and finds its way to the nearest coarse grass or herbaceous vegetation, in our case several feet away from the pond, and here the beautiful adult struggles out of its shining brown jacket. If our pond was surrounded by nothing but mown grass or tarmac, then the darter's habitat would be incomplete and it would probably fail to breed.

There must be a great many examples of species with a dependence on two or more distinct habitats for their survival. Even in a small garden it is possible to provide a considerable variety, with climber-covered walls, clumps of long grass, densely planted flower borders and a pond of fresh water. Each habitat is valuable and fascinating in its own right, but if you create a diversity of habitats, then the wildlife rewards can be even more exciting.

GETTING INVOLVED

12

Having your own private patch is great fun, and very rewarding. Sooner or later, though, you will want to do much more than just observe your neighbourhood. I hope you'll want to influence the habitats in the wildlife network beyond your garden fence, and there is endless enjoyment to be had in sharing nature with other interested people.

More often than not, it will be a sudden wildlife crisis that brings you out of the garden, and unites you with your 'green neighbours'. It may be an article in the local paper, announcing the plan to build a new supermarket 'on derelict wasteland', or it may be something much more immediate – such as the sudden arrival of a 'cowboy tree-lopper' and the sickening sound of infernal power saws, eating away at your local songbird habitat. There is nothing quite like a chainsaw massacre to rally the troops.

If you're faced with an immediate crisis then the first thing you must do is find someone to support you. Then whilst one of you pleads with the agents of destruction, the other can get on the phone and activate the alarm system. In urban areas we are really rather lucky. Whilst countryside conservationists may, for the time being at least, be powerless to act against the local landowners, in towns we have democratic decision-making. Thanks to our highly sophisticated system of environmental controls and planning, most major changes have first to be considered and authorised by the public, working through elected councillors and their paid professional officers. So – back to the chainsaw massacre. While the more reasonable and mild of the two of you quietly and calmly lies down in front of the digger, or valiantly embraces the nearest tree, with tears streaming and perhaps the odd fiver changing hands, Green Guerrilla number two should phone your first line of emergency contact – the planning department of the local

Mass community tree planting is a great way to establish the idea that conservation is 'politically popular'. Make sure the press and councillors are invited.

council. Ask to be put through to the 'planner' who deals with the area in question, and then explain the nature of the crisis. One of three answers will then emerge. If you are lucky, the destruction taking place will be without the knowledge or consent of the planners, and they should immediately send someone to investigate. If you are very unlucky, they will know all about it, having given planning approval for it to take place, and you will simply have missed the boat. You then need to ask yourself why you didn't comment when the permission was being considered – but more of that later.

A third possibility is that the destructive activity you are so angry about is beyond the control of planners. Regrettably this applies to a great deal of habitat destruction. Your trees, for instance, will only be protected under special circumstances when they are the subject of a tree preservation order or stand within an official conservation area. The burning off of bramble scrub by British Rail is considered to be part of normal embankment management, though they are now beginning to adopt a closed season at nesting time, and restrict the use of weedkillers. The most upsetting kind of destruction is that done in the misguided name of 'environmental improvement'. As a landscape architect myself, it makes me shudder to think how many 'landscaping schemes' become a well-meant excuse for replacing rich, tangled wildlife habitat with sterile green desert, tarmac and lollipop trees. Job creation all too often means habitat destruction.

Phoning the planning office is all very well from 9.30 to 4.30, Monday to Friday, but your five-star cowboys know very well that they will have less aggravation if they fell the protected trees outside office hours. It is quite remarkable, too, how often listed buildings seem mysteriously to collapse at bank holiday weekends, when no one is looking. If the power saws wake you on a Sunday morning, then your life-line outside office hours is the local councillor, and I strongly recommend you bring in the local police for good measure. They may not wish to 'get involved' but they are obliged to drop in, if only to avert the breach of the peace you have in mind, and if there is any doubt in a cowboy's mind, he'll be off like a shot the minute the cavalry appear on the horizon.

If your crisis is one of 'official authorised destruction', misguided 'environmental improvement', in other words, then you will have to take a different, more diplomatic route. By all means try to persuade the parks worker or the railway ganger, but as likely as not you'll be up against the famous

British 'Jobsworth' problem. You may well find the destruction team is genuinely concerned, but they are just following orders, and the best you can expect is that they will work more slowly, or find something else to do whilst you talk to 'the boss'.

People seem to have a very pessimistic view of 'the council' and 'the management' but in my experience, most people in authority are keen to sort out problems amicably. Certainly in the case of publicly-owned land I find that managers are rather pleased to have members of the public showing any interest at all, and will generally hold up operations until there has been a chance to talk. The secret really is for you to remain polite, calm and positive – but obviously determined, and you must be prepared to listen too. British Rail may argue that they have no option but to clear scrub periodically in order to keep the railway safe, but if you are reasonable yourself they may equally well be prepared to stop all such destruction until the following winter, when it will do the least amount of damage. Once you have established a calm relationship with the regional office, there can be spin-offs too. In Islington, British Rail have allowed access to a particularly wild stretch of embankment, for use as a schools' nature reserve, and in Birmingham there are plans for a stretch of cutting to be declared a wildlife sanctuary, and positively managed to favour butterflies and birds.

Remember! We own British Rail. The way this marvellous wildlife resource is managed depends on us.

When it comes to the local council, then you can be much more optimistic about a positive outcome to your campaign. This land is your land, very definitely, and if you are persuasive, and can show that your opinion is a popular one, then local councillors and their staff really are obliged to take it seriously. The key here is to be realistic, and to demonstrate the popularity of your ideas. Don't press immediately for a policy of afforestation on the local football pitches, or introducing frogspawn to the park paddling pools. Begin modestly, with requests for a patch or two of mini-meadow, for instance, and support your requests with letters from other ratepayers, and genuine offers of help. If you agree to organise the hay-raking, provided they stop spraying and agree to cut in July and September only, then generally speaking you will be made very welcome. Community haymaking is already an established fact in the parks of Birmingham, Bristol, Swindon and London.

In Birmingham, my Urban Wildlife Group colleagues and I dreamed up a very clever way of persuading the parks department to begin thinking about meadows in parks. We

wrote to the director, telling him that we wanted to hold an
international daisy-chain championship and asking if his staff
would provide us with an acre of daisies to be in flower for
the second week of May. We had no doubt that the parks staff
could deliver the goods. After all, they had been getting into
trouble for years whenever the daisies got 'out of control'.
The bargain was struck. We organised teams of competitors
from lots of local schools, the councillors came to have their
photos taken surrounded by happy little future ratepayers
(and civic chains of daisies) and almost overnight wildflowers
became acceptable in parks.

Don't be put off by officials who tell you that the public
demand neat and tidy deserts. Remember that you are 'the
public' too. In fact, what the officers and politicians mean by
'the public' is the very small number of moaners who bother to
write and complain. Often you will find that as few as half a
dozen negative but persistent complainers are shaping landscape
policy for a whole city. Just make sure in future that there is
always a bigger pile of letters in praise of the longer grass,
the fallen leaves, the dead branches on trees, the nettle patches
and the wildflowers. Changing official policy really is as
simple as that.

You can be encouraged, too, by the fact that some properly
structured research shows that most people would in fact
love to see more wildflowers in parks. They want more
'undergrowth', more songbirds, more nature on their
doorstep. Researchers at University College, London, took
five sample groups of people living in different districts of
the London Borough of Greenwich. They talked and talked
about what they wanted from their parks and open spaces,
and it seemed, in fact, that no one was in favour of close-mown
grass and lollipop trees. Just because the moaners and the
tidiers up have always taken the trouble to complain, we've
been given an official landscape which very few people actually
seem to want. It is high time you and I made our feelings
known. The wildlife, and the local kids, would be very grateful.

Building up a close relationship with the major land
managers in your area must be the real key to successful
campaigns in the longer term, and to do that you need to
establish some sort of authority yourself. The British are
great joiners, so why not simply organise a gathering of some
kind, on a conservation theme, and advertise it locally? The
people who turn up will form the core of your local wildlife
group. I think it is best if this event is something very positive

– a litter clear-up around the local pond, a hay-making party
in the park, a hedgerow-planting session around the edge
of the school field. All these types of activity will appeal to the
kind of folk who want to do practical, physical things for
conservation. You need to appeal to the not-so-active, too,
and whilst the obvious way to attract them might be a wildlife
slide-talk, or a RSPB film show, there are other, more subtle
ideas you might try. Why not put out a call for old photographs
showing the neighbourhood before the war? Ask for
home-made nest-boxes that can be erected in the local park
or churchyard. Launch a neighbourhood wildlife survey and
ask for volunteers who are prepared to plot their own
immediate surroundings.

If all pleas for enthusiastic support seem to fall on deaf ears,
no one turns up to your hay-making party, and you finish
up planting the entire hedgerow yourself, then you could be
really devious, and adopt the ultimate Green Guerrilla tactic.
Start a rumour. Choose the patch of green, leafy wildlife
habitat that you know everyone in your neighbourhood really
loves, and invent a threat to it. A few well chosen whispers in
the bus queue, the chip shop and the supermarket checkout
should do the trick. 'Shame all the trees in the churchyard
have got to come down', or 'Fancy building houses in the
Dingle – where will the kids play now?' – I'm sure you get the
idea. If that tactic doesn't work, then I suggest you move
house and leave your neighbours to be slowly engulfed in a
sea of concrete, tarmac and litter.

The main purpose of 'forming a group' is to help justify
regular consultation with the decision-makers in the parks
department and elsewhere in the council. That way you should
be forewarned of most of the future crises long before they
happen, and indeed you will be able to start making positive
suggestions too. To be taken seriously you do have to be
reliable, and that means choosing representatives who can be
easily contacted, and you must be prepared to compromise.
Don't be too quick to back down, though. You are there to
represent the wildlife in your area. It is up to other interest
groups to argue for their particular point of view.

In 1980, I helped to form a local voluntary organisation
called the Urban Wildlife Group, with the intention of
championing wildlife in Birmingham and the Black Country.
Five years later there were over forty similar groups, in
towns and cities as far apart as Plymouth and Glasgow,
Norwich and Swansea. We now have regular meetings with

Keeping up the enthusiasm is not quite so easy. This hedge-bank has been built by volunteers on the site of the New Victoria Theatre in the Potteries. You've got to be very keen to work on a wet Sunday in January, and to keep on turning up year after year. In this case the continuing enthusiasm of Peter Cheeseman, the Theatre's Director, has produced an amazing voluntary effort, and a very special urban wildlife landscape.

most of the land managers in our area. The planning officers send us details of every single planning application in plenty of time for us to visit the site and comment on the proposals, and perhaps most importantly, all those ordinary folk who care about the wildlife right on their doorstep now have someone they can contact the minute they hear a rumour of some threatened destruction. The Urban Wildlife Group has grown dramatically, and by sponsoring a large government-funded employment scheme we now have a team of qualified ecologists, planners, landscape architects, graphic designers, teachers and office staff – a formidable force for conservation which simply has to be taken seriously. We have over four thousand supporters, thanks to an arrangement which encourages local people to buy a badge and become an official supporter for life. That demonstration of public popularity is all the encouragement the politicians need, in order to justify a more naturalistic approach to the management of parks, road verges and school grounds.

Now, supposing you have an ear to the ground, you spot an official announcement in the library or the local paper, or the planning watchdogs in your group get wind of a proposed development – one that is going through the legitimate channels of planning control. The first thing to do is find out the facts. Every planning application has to be entered in the public planning register, and there is a period of at least three weeks during which the application must be available for public viewing, and when formal objections can be lodged. If you want to influence, or in some cases prevent development, then you must act quickly. Firstly you must put together the most thorough and factual written objection you can, supported by as many signatures as possible. This means looking closely at the site, and using all those techniques we talked about in chapter five, to show how important the site is in the broader local landscape. Show that the length of ditch which would be culverted in the proposed scheme is in fact a vital corridor link for kingfishers travelling between the park lake and the derelict canal area. Show that the mature oak tree is an important landmark for everyone in the area, and dates back to the days when your town was just a tiny village. By all means include the most comprehensive species-list you can muster. All those Latin names of obscure wild plants and insects will certainly make 'em think twice – but do beware. If you baffle the decision-makers with too much science, they will write you off as elitist cranks and you will lose the fight. There is no doubt that certain types of wildlife have much more political appeal than others. There is something I call 'the orchid factor' which can be very powerful indeed. Everyone wants to feel they are saving something rare, so orchids are a buzz word. Some species are just generally more appealing than others. Kingfishers score ten out of ten, with owls, squirrels and robins well up towards the top of the charts. Grass-snakes are definitely an acquired taste, and best mentioned only to the converted, whilst rats, cockroaches and slugs are somewhere way down below the bottom of the chart. Remember that, to most people, those interesting, furry small mammals you find so fascinating are just a load of vermin, but the kestrels which feed on them are seen by everyone as 'wonderful wildlife'. Lots of signatures on a petition certainly add weight to your case, but there is no doubt that individual letters from ratepayers count for much more. A bundle of ten letters is impressive. A petition with a hundred signatures tends to draw attention to all those people who *didn't* sign. Do press your supporters to write. It really does make a surprisingly big difference. Give them all the details of where to write to, when to get their letter in by and the main points you suggest they make – but don't write a standard letter for them to sign – that would be no better than a single petition.

When it comes to saving wildlife, there is no better tactic than to drag the decision-makers down into the depths of the landscape, and bring them face to face with the wildlife you are trying to save. Any attempt to win the case on paper is no substitute for direct contact. I remember taking a group of planning committee members to visit a patch of beautiful wet woodland which was threatened with house-building, and on another occasion some very parochial parish councillors were themselves threatening to chop down a small wood to make way for a children's play area. In the case of the housing site, we managed to choose a day in late May, when the birds should have been singing, and the flowers should have been decorating the sun-dappled glades. Unfortunately it poured with rain, but because the planners had hired a coach for the day, and we had amassed a selection of wellies, they had little option but to wade in. My heart sunk as these city fathers chuntered and grumbled their way down the bank, getting wetter by the minute as dripping twigs slapped them across the face, and wet grass soaked their skirts and

This lovely old tree is doomed to die. Keep a close eye on planning applications, and if you move quickly enough this kind of short-sighted destruction can sometimes be avoided.

trousers. Once inside, however, the woodland and its wildlife worked a magical spell. As we all stood dripping amongst the trees, the chairman spotted a tiny frog, hopping through the wet grass at his feet. In no time at all the entire committee was bounding around after froglets, reliving their childhood and understanding absolutely why we all felt the place was so special. As the bedraggled party struggled breathlessly back to the bus, they talked of nothing else but the outrageous proposal to destroy such a smashing place, and we knew the wildlife had won.

The threat of the parish play area was even more amusing. There was money available to lay tarmac, put up football posts, build a few swings, and generally provide 'an amenity' for local children. The problem was that the chosen site, although designated as a play space on the county map, was actually covered in mature willows and long grass, and had a delightful stream flowing through it. The councillors grudgingly agreed to pay a visit before finally giving the go-ahead, and at first all their worst fears were confirmed. This was an untidy site, with dangerously steep slopes, deep mud and open water – a veritable death-trap to their parishioners. As I valiantly argued that it had survived for a very long time without mishap, and weakly threw in the odd plea for the woodpeckers and water rail, who should emerge from the undergrowth but a gang of half a dozen junior parishioners. These handy representatives of the local youth were invited over, and in the best tradition of unbiased opinion polls, the councillors asked if they would like a super new play area with all the very best equipment. The kids were visibly appalled. 'What's wrong with the place as it is?' they said. One lad even had a pair of binoculars round his neck and was eager to show the councillors the list of birds he'd seen. The councillors were confused. Here were people recreating without any formal provision. How remarkable! Needless to say, the kids saved the day. Instead of becoming a sterile play area, the site survived as a fabulous natural play area, and again the wildlife heaved a sigh of relief.

Don't be blinkered in your championing on site. You are very unlikely to win the day purely on grounds of 'interesting wildlife'. Look for fellow supporters with other axes to grind. One of the most powerful arguments for conservation is 'education'. Involve the local school and make the point very forcibly to the planners that this is a landscape where children play, and where they can learn about nature.

There may be straight planning objections to the threatened development which you should support, too. Remember that the planning officers are public servants, there to give you professional advice, and certainly not simply to represent the applicant who wishes to develop. Ask if the new industrial estate will lead to traffic problems. Can the sewage system cope with all these new houses? Does yet another retail warehouse or super-supermarket fit in with the local planning strategy for the area, or will it destroy business in the High Street? The more points you can add to your case, the stronger will be your chances.

Do try to find a friend at court, too. There are certain to be local councillors, members of the planning committee, who will champion your point of view. At the very least they will see environmental conservation as a popular bandwagon, and many of them will genuinely share your concern. They will have colleagues on the committee that they can 'get at' and with luck you can have won the day before the decision-makers even meet.

If, after refusal, the developer decides 'to go to appeal', then the local children are again vitally important allies, largely because no one ever thinks to canvass their opinion, and you can. When a developer appeals against a planning refusal, the decision is reconsidered at a higher level. The Minister of State for the Environment appoints a representative, called a planning inspector, who listens to all interested parties, and then passes judgement. If you or your group objected formally to the original application, then you should automatically be invited to put your point of view to the inspector at this public enquiry. Sometimes, for minor developments, the whole consultation exercise is carried out by letter, with the inspector considering the case on the basis of written evidence only. It is almost always in your best interests to press for a hearing in public. This way the inspector is faced with real people, and will get a much better feel for the emotional commitment of locals. If you do get stuck with 'written evidence only', then you must make sure that everybody bothers to write. Remember there is usually only one developer, so the fact that you can counter with a pile of letters really is taken seriously.

In any event, the inspector is bound to visit and inspect the site in question. Do try and wangle yourself an invitation, so that you can make sure your point of view is heard on site, and do everything possible to get that visit timed for a part

Don't forget 'the orchid factor'. Support your case with the kind of threatened wildlife everyone wants to save. Owls are OK. The rats and mice they depend upon are best left unmentioned.

of the year when the wildlife value is obvious. You are much more likely to win the day after a visit in May, than if the inspection is forced to take place in February, when everyone is cold and miserable, and the bluebells, may blossom and nightingales are little more than a gleam in your eye. If that does happen, take photos along to show the inspector how much prettier the site looks in the sun. If you are fortunate, and the enquiry is in public, then you must persuade as many local supporters as possible to attend, and do make sure that lots of the neighbours stand up and state their case. Don't worry too much about reasoned and structured arguments. In many ways a genuine emotional outburst about 'the poor trees' or 'our local hedgehog' is much better than a formal, prepared statement. This is where the local children come in. The Urban Wildlife Group has succeeded at several public enquiries by adopting a two-pronged attack. We have presented a formal report which contains the *objective* arguments, with lists of species, notes of council minutes, photographs of the site at different seasons, etc. The secret ingredient in this winning report, however, is not cold, calm and objective at all. We always try to include short quotations from local people, and children in particular, which simply express their feelings about the place. On one page we may have notes of council decisions which were made at poorly-attended meetings and which therefore weaken the opposition's case – but the local kids are included too and on the page opposite there will be a quotation which says something like 'the snails that live there are my friends' – Karen, aged 8. Believe me, with friends like Karen, those snails are pretty safe.

Urban nature conservation isn't just a matter of getting up the nose of everyone who wants to build in your local wildscape – far from it. Having staggered this far through the book I hope you will have lots of ideas you want to put into practice, and incidentally, offering ideas for positive alternatives to development, and volunteering practical help with implementation too, is another powerful argument for your case at public enquiries.

Assuming that you have managed to stop the threat of development once and for all, or that you have identified a barren gap in your habitat network which needs improving, how do you get involved with practical conservation? Quite often, the site you have your eye on will not have been the subject of a planning tussle. It will just be a vacant patch you fancy helping. First of all, remember that all land belongs to someone, somewhere, and however neglected and unloved it may seem, you must gain permission before you get stuck in. Finding out who owns land in the town can be very, very difficult. Sometimes it is obvious, of course. A big sign which says 'British Rail Property – Keep Out' means you need look no further. If there is no such helpful label on your site, try asking neighbouring landowners. They can often give you a clue. Failing that, then it is back to the planning office at the local council. Because every planning application for the past thirty odd years has been registered by law, the planners now have an amazing record of all those applications, and even if your particular site has not itself been the subject of an application, the owners may well have been contacted, or have commented in connection with an application for an adjacent site. There will also be a record of all the council-owned land and they themselves may well own the plot next door. This could be a clue to the ownership of your site. If you pursue these various avenues you will then be very unlucky if you don't throw up anything useful, though your first piece of information may well be out of date, and there could be many more letters and telephone calls before you finally track down the current owner.

If you want to visit the site, or to offer to help carry out habitat management of some kind, then you have to have the legal authority to be there, and this can be achieved in three ways. In all three it is useful to have the help and advice of a lawyer, though a well-established local group may well have volunteers who are solicitors, or the local authority may be prepared to provide you with free legal advice.

The most powerful and secure authority you can have over the land is ownership. In the countryside, rural conservationists spend hundreds of thousands of pounds every year, buying up fragments of rich habitat to ensure near-absolute protection. In the town that is almost never going to be possible. Land costs are influenced by the value of industrial or housing development, and are way beyond the reach of most people. Having said that, some urban wildlife groups are becoming owners of city land, because generous benefactors offer it to them at bargain prices. For the most part, though, landownership is very unlikely. You are much more likely to agree to rent the land in question. By signing a *lease* you have full possession of the site for an agreed length of time. Generally you will assume a good deal of legal responsibility upon signing, and you will be expected to treat the land responsibly, since it does not actually belong to you. A lease does imply payment of some kind, though if you are in luck, and the owner is generous, the cost may be nominal – a peppercorn rent. Once you sign a lease, you do have exclusive possession of the land, without interference from the landlord, but you will be expected to take responsibility for the maintenance and upkeep of the property. It will almost certainly pay dividends if you involve the owner in your project as far as possible. Although you have the legal right to independence, an invitation to the owner to join a management committee is likely to ease the problem of negotiating conditions into the lease, and may well reduce the rent too.

As a tenant you will have the right to be served a 'notice to quit' the land, and the period of that notice forms a negotiated part of the lease. Six months is probably convenient for both parties, since it will give you long enough to see the nesting season through if nest-boxes are occupied, for example, whilst at the same time being short enough to keep up morale as you dismantle your involvement.

Apart from the upkeep of all features of the land which are not expressly excluded in the detail of the lease, you will have other legal responsibilities too. You are now the 'occupier' and as such you must make sure that anyone who enters the land lawfully is *reasonably* safe. You are not responsible for the safety of trespassers, but it is important to realise that trespassers must know they are trespassing. Simply putting up a sign which says 'Private, access only with permission', is of little use if the trespassers can enter without seeing the notice, or if they are children too young to read.

If you actually invite people on to the site, then you are certainly responsible for their well-being. If you know they are coming, you can ask them to sign a note accepting that they enter at their own risk, but that does not excuse you from making their visit 'reasonably safe' and in the eyes of the law, something as innocent as the building of a footbridge, or the erection of an unlocked gate in the fence is likely to be interpreted as an invitation.

However careful you are, and however seriously you take your legal responsibilities, wild areas attract kids. You will inevitably have young children entering your site whether you like it or not. They deserve a special mention. If there are serious hazards on the site, you do have a moral as well as a legal responsibility to put up some kind of physical barrier, or remove the hazard. In the case of a hazard such as a poisonous plant, you have a peculiar responsibility, since as a nature conservationist you will be treated as an expert and assumed to know the extent of the threat poisonous plants pose. At the end of the day, when the site has been fenced and signposted, visitors have signed an acceptance of personal responsibility, volunteer wardens have patrolled the paths, and every other reasonable precaution has been taken, please insure against personal accident liability. Insurance will not remove all your responsibilities, and a cash payment is poor compensation for a broken leg, or worse. The insurers will still expect you to take care of the site, but it should mean that you can retain the basic character of your wildlife site, and not be forced to adopt the very techniques of landscape sterilisation which probably drove you to get involved in the first place.

In many cases you will not need anything as elaborate or exclusive as a lease, in order to enjoy the wildlife on your site. If you simply need authority to carry out a wildflower survey, to watch birds, or perhaps visit occasionally with a group of schoolchildren, then you should aim to negotiate a *licence*. This gives you express permission to enter the site to undertake specific activities. Again it is a legally binding document, but you are unlikely to be asked for anything more than nominal payment, and most importantly you do not become responsible for the site as a whole. A 'bare' licence involves no payment, but the permission can be withdrawn at any time. A licence by deed gives more security, and may, for instance, include the agreement of a 'minimum notice to quit', but as a consequence it will generally involve a payment.

Although as a licensee you are not expected to carry any responsibility for repairs or maintenance to property, you are still responsible for those people you invite on to the land in the exercise of your licence.

Once you have legal access to your site, you will want to start work immediately. Do please remember that over-enthusiasm can be a mistake. Live with the site for a while, and learn how it works in detail. A hollow which you write off as a boring patch of grass in the autumn, and earmark for instant tree-planting, may in fact fill up with water each winter, and be the ancestral spawning ground for all the local frogs. The patch of straggly, brown bracken you fancy converting into a wildflower meadow could support a sheet of bluebells in the spring, dependent for their success on the shade from the fern-fronds.

The ideal pattern for getting more people involved, would be to wait until the end of your first summer, when you have had a chance to see just how your fellow locals use the site. Is it a bike trail in the school holidays? Does everyone dump their lawn clippings there?

At the end of the summer holidays, when the nights are drawing in, organise a litter clearance party. Tell the local school, leaflet all the nearby neighbours, and make sure that you provide plastic collecting sacks, and perhaps a skip from the council if the rubbish is bulky. Try and borrow a few pairs of heavy duty gloves, too. Choose a Saturday or Sunday, for obvious reasons, and try to avoid a date that clashes with other local events. A home football match or a local fête can decimate your work force. Take time off through the day to talk to the whole group of helpers, and to begin explaining the site and its habitats, and if you don't feel confident enough to do that yourself, see if you can find a local 'expert' who can do the job. The conservation organisations in your area should

This little patch of wet woodland was threatened by council plans for a childrens' play area . . .

be able to help. Mention through the day that you are
looking for a small group of people to take a special interest
in the site, to visit it regularly, keep an eye on it, and to build
up the wildlife records. The folk who live overlooking the site
will make excellent security guards, and you will probably
find one or two knowledgeable locals keen to do a plant survey,
or keep records of the nesting birds. Once this core of 'friends'
is established, it will be much easier to decide what really
needs to be done.

I suggest you always try to involve the local schools if
possible. Offer to show groups of children round the site,
or even better, show the teachers round on their own first,
and they are quite likely to provide you with some really
helpful supporters. Once you have the confidence of the
neighbourhood, then it is time to put up a simple notice,
somewhere obvious, giving the site a name, and asking (not
telling) people to take care of the wildlife. If there are plenty
of visitors already, and you have found your volunteer wardens,

Local people saved it, and now it is a nature reserve – but the local children are certainly not complaining. They know there is room for them AND the wildlife.

then one very successful idea you should try, is to put up a simple notice board in which you can display current information about the wildlife on site. The notice board obviously needs to be weatherproof and substantial with an unbreakable perspex front to it, and I suggest that the first things you put in there are the drawings and poems that children from the local junior and infant schools produce. Provide a contact address for news of 'sightings', and then keep the information changing, with cut-out pictures of the birds people see, the butterflies that are around in summer, and the wildflowers as they come into bloom. It does make a difference to people's enjoyment to know that the flocks of LBJs (little brown jobs) up on the alder trees are probably redpoll and siskin on migration from Scandinavia, and there is great satisfaction in knowing the difference between red admiral and small tortoiseshell butterflies. This simple 'postbox' system really does build up people's confidence quickly. When we first erected the notice board on our local wet woodland patch, all the entries were provided by so-called 'experts' but pretty soon there were reports coming in of a tawny owl, and then a green woodpecker, a sparrow hawk, and then a kingfisher. Once the sightings were checked out, or two or three people came up with the same story, a suitable picture was found for the notice board, and more and more people began to take a serious interest. I was particularly pleased when one local teenager turned up with some wonderful pen and ink drawings of butterflies that he'd produced specially.

Having said that, one of the biggest dangers in all this 'conservation' is that the whole thing becomes terribly earnest. For goodness sake don't let your enthusiasm for wildlife squeeze everyone else out of the landscape. There is no place in the town for exclusive wildlife ghettos. Your whole aim should be to provide easy access and casual enjoyment for all those millions of people who are *not* fanatics. It must be possible for people just to walk the dog, sneak off for a cuddle or build a den, whilst still providing a safe habitat for our wildlife. Try and make sure your site remains full of life of all kinds. In that way we will gradually shake off the idea that nature conservation is elitist, middle class and boring. The real joy of the wild side of towns is direct contact with the delights of the commonplace. There is no future for the nature in the city if we constantly try to ram it down everybody's throats.

REAL JOBS IN CONSERVATION

13

The most persuasive word in the English language today is
jobs. No matter how devastating the proposals to build on
a wild green site may be, if the developers suggest that
they can create new jobs then they are home and dry. Most
of their promises are complete eyewash, but they offer hope
to desperate politicians faced with soaring unemployment.
It's an offer they can't refuse. If we are to stem this tide of
pointless destruction, then the conservation lobby must start
to blow its own trumpet as far as job creation is concerned.

The propaganda from the destruction lobby is terribly well
rehearsed. They can tell you with an absolutely straight face,
exactly how many hundreds of thousands of *new* jobs their
latest grotesque cluster of warehouses will create. They say,
of course, that they can only possibly work their miracle if we
allow them green fields to build on, and a relaxation in the
planning controls that might otherwise stifle their enterprise.

I've watched the process enough times now to recognise it
for what it really is – callous, selfish greed. With oceans of
capital sloshing about in the economy, land and buildings are
still considered to be a worthwhile investment despite the
fact that there are millions of square feet of commercial floor
space standing idle. The new warehouses and factory units are
little more than krugerrands with roofs on. It matters little to
the speculators whether they ever find a tenant. The
buildings are an adequate currency in themselves, and it is so
much cheaper and and easier to build on a green, virgin site
than to reclaim the ugly dereliction left by the last generation
of 'entrepreneurs'.

Before we begin looking to our own laurels as
environmentalists, it is worth a brief review of the real job
creation record of the destruction lobby. I have a
government-sponsored Enterprize Zone close to me, built
largely on the site of a fifty-acre working farm. I am told by

Plenty of young people long for a job 'helping nature'. Caring for the landscape could create huge numbers of jobs, improve the environment, and benefit the balance of payments, too.

the propagandists that the enterprising industrialists who are moving into the giant multi-coloured short-life sheds are the 'wealth-creators' of society. I apparently owe them a vote of thanks for providing me and my kind with the wherewithal to indulge my non-productive interests.

The biggest of the new buildings are retail warehouses. Their low staffing-levels, fork-lift trucks and computerised stock control are combining to drive the High Street shopkeepers out of business and kill off the centres of surrounding towns.

Most of the smaller units are occupied by 'new businesses' which have transferred from older premises a mile or so away, often conveniently shedding employees in the move. More often than not they operate as importers or wholesalers of some kind, buying in foreign goods, marking up the price, possibly screwing the parts together, and then selling them on to people like you and me. Their kind of 'wealth-earning' is a direct negative drain on the nation's economy, yet they are fawned over by politicians and given all kinds of publicly funded incentives to expand their drain-power. It is high time society came to its senses, and stopped believing the hollow propagandist promises of jobs tomorrow in exchange for environmental quality today. The progress in environmental controls that we have achieved over the past forty years is being thrown away in a mad scramble to please the 'enterprising developers' and no one seems to be prepared to point out that these particular kings have no clothes.

By contrast, a more caring society can provide a wealth of worthwhile employment for people. Conservation is already a huge employer, and contributes a great deal to the balance of payments. It is high time we began to stand up and be counted.

Since 1970, there has been a dramatic growth in the number of people employed directly in the environmental industry. Even in the narrow field of nature conservation there is an ever-increasing band of wardens, professional lobbyists, landscape architects, ecologists, nursery workers and contractors making a living from wildlife. Casting the net a little more widely, whole industries have sprung up as a result of the public's growing concern for the environment. All those garden ponds are lined with a waterproof membrane that someone manufactured. There are nurseries growing wildflowers, and packeting seed. There are millions of pounds worth of binoculars and photographic gear sold to nature-lovers

every year, wellies and shovels, mechanical diggers,
bird-boxes, bird hides, natural history books and a host of other
products, all being made and sold to help the money go round,
and the world to become a little greener.

Those direct spin-offs are only the tip of the iceberg.
Tourism is now the second biggest earner of foreign
currency in Britain. For the most part it is conservationists
who cater for that market. Few tourists come to admire our
industrial estates, our hypermarkets or our urban sprawl. They
want to enjoy the history tied up in our landscapes and our
buildings, and most of that heritage is fast diminishing, thanks
to the destructive urge of the ever-popular wealth-earning
development sector.

Now I've got that off my chest, perhaps we should look at
the scope I see for positive promotion of employment in

*These tough young lads worked all
weekend to build a wildlife garden
from demolition materials, just to
please the local pensioners.
We must stop valuing this kind of
work less highly than
'manufacturing'. Remember that
assembling imported space-invader
machines is 'manufacturing' but
the jobs created make neither
economic nor social sense.*

conservation. As society begins to value the environment more highly, there are many ways in which the employment of more people would pay dividends. Already, there is a vast work force beavering away, either in their spare time if they happen to have a paid job, or as a means of productively passing the time if they happen to be without paid work. There is a middle-aged man I know, with a wife and teenage family, who left the coal-mining industry after the 1984–85 strike, and has been 'unemployed' ever since. He keeps very busy, caring for a local wildlife site five minutes from home. He is a keen fisherman, and organises the fishing club. He visits the scrub woodland every day through the winter, to feed the wild birds, and spends a pound a week of his social security money on stale bread, seed and fat, so that other visitors can enjoy the sight of woodpeckers, bramblings, siskins, and a great many more common birds, feeding in the sanctuary area. Throughout the summer holidays and most weekends he works with the local kids, and together they have built fishing platforms, fences, footbridges and benches throughout their landscape. After years underground he now knows exactly how he wants to spend the rest of his working life. His value to that community is enormous. He improves the quality of numerous people's lives, and he is happy. How sensible it would be for society to provide him, and many others like him, with a respectable living wage.

There is already considerable movement in this direction, of course. The various temporary employment schemes go some way towards financing a great deal of this kind of caring work, but the essential weakness in the schemes as they stand, is that they offer only short-term security, and the landscape demands long-term commitment. The government says that temporary schemes give far more unemployed people 'a taste of work'. The cynics say that longer term unemployment schemes will never be popular with the government because they have less impact on the statistical reduction in the numbers of long-term unemployed.

I have been intimately involved in a major employment scheme for several years now. The Urban Wildlife Group has been able to employ over three hundred staff in five years, thanks to central and local government financing schemes. The Manpower Services Commission are looking all the time for individuals or groups of people who will sponsor a scheme. You don't have to be an 'expert' to apply. You just

need to have a good idea for making positive use of
employees to improve the environment. They pay the wages
– you could be coming up with the ideas. There is no doubt
that the energy, enthusiasm and skill of all the people on our
scheme has made an enormous difference to our rate of
progress in caring for the wild landscapes of the Midlands,
but it is so frustrating to see that despite the valuable work
they do, when their twelve months are up they must leave,
and a new batch of raw recruits will begin inventing the
wheel all over again. Many return to the dole queue, although
we do have a better than average record of people moving
on into properly paid and permanent posts. Many who go back
on the dole continue to work for UWG voluntarily, and if
they are under twenty-five, then six months later they can
change statistical columns and begin to be paid again. If
they're over twenty-five, the required gap is twelve months.
In many ways, this kind of employment is superb. For a
young, idealistic graduate there could be nothing better than
to work in a position of responsibility, surrounded by other
equally self-motivated young people, co-operating within a
team of many skills. At present though, there is no career
on offer, and once twenty-five arrives, and responsibilities
mount, the prospect of twelve months on/twelve months off
for minimal pay is heart-breaking. There must be many a
middle-aged industrial worker who, like my redundant
miner, would love to leave the work bench and spend ten or
fifteen years in the fresh air, working with children, caring
for the natural environment, or perhaps applying the
craftsmanship of a skilled hobby to renovation of old buildings
or managing the landscape. If the system were changed
slightly, the environment would benefit from that reservoir
of experience, maturity and expertise, and the young
could more readily be accommodated in industrial careers.

I must say I am very optimistic. It makes such obvious
common sense to occupy people in creative, worthwhile,
caring work. A greener, pleasanter environment is healthier,
more attractive to other more orthodox industries, and it
enhances the dollar-earning capacity of tourism too. It surely
won't be long now before we all accept that the long-awaited,
post-industrial era has at last arrived. We must stop talking
depressingly about the three-day week and start welcoming
in the long-awaited four-day weekend. Whilst the whizz-kids
of high technology and their computerised robotic mates get
on with the tedious job of manufacturing, and earning wealth,

the rest of us can hold our heads up high, and work away at all those valuable tasks we always wished we had time for.

In the short term, our only hope of becoming respectable and being taken seriously seems to be to make a financial profit from conservation, and here too there are some very exciting developments afoot. Several of the people who have completed a year with the Urban Wildlife Group, for instance, have gone on to set up their own companies. An ecologist and a planner have joined forces to offer commercial consultancy to local authorities, industrialists and community groups. A group of nursery and landscape workers have set up a contracting business to build wildlife gardens for the public. It is only a matter of time before a specialist chain of garden centres opens, where concerned gardeners can buy organic gardening gear, native trees and shrubs, approved nest-box designs, wild bird food, pond liners, and all the other paraphernalia which at present is forced to sit unhappily alongside shelves of garden pesticides. With a little of that entrepreneurial enterprise I was so cynical about earlier, there must be many more genuine, commercial jobs to be invented, and if we really do become broadly conservation-conscious in Britain, there is enormous scope for employment in recycling industries, building insulation, labour intensive organic farming, pollution control technology and so on.

Finally, there is the scope for productive wildscape. You will remember my plea for urban forestry in chapter ten. Commercial coppicing could fuel the local economy in more ways than one. Those gravel pits and reservoirs could be fish-farmed, the parks meadows could support livestock too, and even the demolition rubble of abandoned industry has cropping potential. Evening primrose and lupins are becoming important agricultural crops, producing highly valued vegetable oil for specialist commercial uses. Both these species thrive on the poorest of rubbly soils, and both can be cropped within a year.

There are *real* jobs in nature conservation. None of them are any less wealth-creating than the vast majority of our hallowed manufacturing industries. Many of them show a direct benefit to the nation's balance of payments, in reducing imports, or boosting tourism. Most importantly of all, they are jobs with fulfilment where individuals can each work close to nature, sharing living experience with other people, conserving our non-renewable resources and making Britain a better, greener, healthier place for future generations to enjoy.

GREEN DREAMS

14

I travel by train as often as I can. Leaving the car at home helps me make a modest little contribution to energy conservation; when they run to time it helps 'take the strain' as the adverts say, and it gives me a privileged view of the wild side of town. On long journeys in particular, I often find myself day dreaming about the landscape of the future, when towns will be ringed by productive woodland, parks will be filled with wildflowers, and people will work and play in a green environment free from harmful chemicals, and full of life.

There's nothing dreamlike about the start of my journeys. City stations do seem to attract more than their fair share of clutter, and even that most hardy of urban creatures, the town pigeon, struts endlessly round and round, as if it has nothing better to do than wait for the next train. There are other glimpses of secret wildlife here, too. I'm always amused to see the mice that scurry busily about their business in the no man's land between the railway sleepers. Presumably they are oblivious to the immense locomotives that wheeze and grunt overhead.

Even the railway carriages themselves are not without their interesting wild residents. There is a famous example of a botanical survey team who discovered a very unusual moss, growing on the window ledges of the London to Bristol railway carriages. They were at a complete loss to know in exactly which kilometre square to plot their mobile rarity.

The stretch of townscape that greets me after the train pulls out of the station is usually particularly grim. In the great days of steam it would have been bustling with activity, but all that ended over thirty years ago, and nothing very positive has happened to most of the redundant railway land since. Certainly there is plenty of pioneer vegetation around. Buddleias and birch trees generally dominate. If this naturalising jungle was encouraged, then every departing train would slip instantly into leafy countryside, but so far the financial controllers and the politicians have refused to let go and the green landscape continues to be suppressed by 'hope value'. As long as accountants insist that there is a chance of development such land will always be overvalued.

On the journey I take most frequently, there seems to be endless ash and concrete. Estate agents' hoardings offer the only real touch of colour, and even these bright symbols of optimism are a mixed blessing. At best they underline the drabness of their surroundings, but at worst their paint is beginning to peel after years of neglect, and that confirms the fact that no one treats their promises seriously any more. The one high spot is a marvellously grand Victorian-Gothic factory. You can still see the name of the original company, carved over the entrance in proud, stone letters. It's been beautifully restored, with brickwork freshly pointed, and a clever choice of colour for the paintwork. It is good to see that one or two of the new craft workshop units are actually in use now. The sound of hammers and pulleys and treadles and wheels rattling and clattering away must amuse the weary ghosts of all those Victorian workers who grafted there so many years ago. The factory has fine terracotta mouldings around its window frames and roof top, and splendid ironwork on its big black gates. In a funny sort of way, all that detail is made to seem even sharper, finer and more 'special', in contrast with the starkly simple vacant new warehouses on either side. The red, white and blue diagonal stripes which scream 'success' from their corrugated cladding, are hardly the most sensitive complement to Victorian Gothic, and the brutal scale of these simple sheds does make the older building look rather like a pop-up plaything, but investors tell us that 'modern hi-tech industry won't look at anything else but single-storey, open-plan units these days', and of course with so much choice, a development needs to be eye-catching, brand-spanking new, and offer some kind of rates exemption too, to stand even the slightest chance of attracting a tenant. In fact most of this particular estate is little more than a multi-coloured mausoleum. One or two units were let right at the start, but the rest have been telling us they are 'available for sale or to let' ever since the last nut and bolt were tightened by the erection gang. The 'landscaping' the planners insisted on as a sop to the environmentalists has mostly disappeared under a sea of dock, thistle and couch-grass – good for goldfinches, but hardly what the landscape architect had in mind. The few businesses that have moved in are already piling their waste in skips around the tarmac car parks, and just this week, the letter 'S' has slipped in the word enterprise, on the sign that identifies this as yet another valiant attempt to help the manufacturing base of industry to 'bottom out'. We are massively over-supplied with commercial premises. I wish someone could explain to me why it makes sense to use public funds to help speculators build even more. A similar size of public investment in urban forestry would transform city living, and create genuinely new jobs – but it wouldn't make fat profits for speculative developers.

Beyond the dull desolation of the inner city, there are rows of houses backing on to the line, their gardens laid out with neat lawns and colourful concrete patios. The piles of junk on our side of the garden fence are, I suppose, another case of 'out of sight, out of mind'. Anyway, once there is a little more leaf-cover on the brambles, most of the plastic and paper will be conveniently invisible for six summer months. Here and there the garden throw-outs have taken root and there is a fortnight or so in late summer each year when this stage of the journey is really rather colourful, with golden rod and Michaelmas daisy sweeping down in drifts towards the line. All this species-rich sanctuary land would be a real asset if only we could rid ourselves of the man-made junk that finds its way there.

At one point, the rows of houses part to allow a junior school to squeeze in. If we're not travelling too fast, it is often possible to catch sight of bright little faces, gazing out from stuffy classrooms, grateful for the diversion we're providing. If the journey coincides with 'break' there is a rush across the tarmac, and those same faces will be peering at closer quarters through the chain-link fence.

Probably it's the older brothers and sisters of those schoolchildren that I've seen quite often through the winter months, standing pale, cold and miserable at the edge of the windswept playing fields. There have been as many as a dozen of them, half-heartedly planting trees in the grass, or driving in the supporting stakes. This must be the fourth or fifth year in a row that dead trees have been taken out, and replaced with more of the same. All over Britain, employment schemes seem to be taking eager young people, and giving them badly planned tasks to do. If we must plant

trees randomly around the towns, with no thought to long-term management, then surely we should at least make sure they are planted so that they survive. Ironically, there is a jolly green signboard, to tell the world that these are government-sponsored work-experience trees, destined to improve the environment. There could be an enormous number of really interesting, creative jobs for young people if we changed the system, stopped letting statisticians dictate policy, and encouraged 'caring' employment. I must confess I sympathise a good deal with the two fingers offered in salute by the gang of demoralised kids as we go staring by.

Probably the most interesting stage in this part of the journey arrives five minutes later, after we've passed through a slightly posher area of housing. The railway is in a cutting a good deal of the time, but even so, you can sense that there are green and leafy gardens up above. At this time of year the blossom of the Japanese cherries looks lovely, and the forest of pencil-slim conifers is all the clue we need to tell us this is semi-detached suburbia. You get a better class of garden rubbish here, too.

The bit of the journey I've been waiting for comes just at the edge of the most recently built housing estate. I can remember when there were crops in the fields here, and neat, mechanically trimmed hedges too. The fields do still exist, but they are much less tidy now. There is always plenty to entertain the passing passenger, nevertheless. These days the crop is Horseyculture. For just a short stretch before we reach the current farming frontier, there are scruffy 'paddocks' of mud and tightly cropped grass, surrounded by the leggy remnants of those once-neat thorn hedges. There are rather more gaps than bushes now, of course. It is fascinating to see the 'folk art' that has developed, as all manner of scrap items are recruited for the patching-up job. I can only assume that the ponies that now graze these fields are particularly good at escaping. The barriers that have been put in their way are ingenious, to say the least. There are bedsteads, of course, and old garage doors, occasional kitchen cabinets, rusty bicycle frames, and an endless tangle of barbed wire to tie the whole lot together. Here and there a mini-gymkhana circuit decorates a 'paddock', with low jumps built from old oil drums and car tyres, and from time to time some quite new material will turn up. At the moment there seems to be an endless supply of those hefty cardboard tubes that carpets are wrapped around in showrooms. They

Work and wildlife can be made to mix. This huge prestigious office block in Zurich is 'dripping' with hawthorn and bramble, and the workers have birdsong outside their windows.

do make quite smart jumps, I suppose, but surely they could be recycled, rather than just thrown away.

Horseyculture architecture is pretty imaginative too. It gets very chilly out here on the edge of the prairie, and even when so many animals are crowded cosily together in one field, there is still a need for some kind of extra shelter. Un-stables would be a good description for these 'structures'. There are one or two of the original farm buildings still surviving, patched together now with fertiliser bags and corrugated iron sheets. There is even one timber building with the kind of split stable-doors that horses are supposed to lean their heads over. Mostly though, the buildings are the shells of one kind of recycled vehicle or another. Biggest of all is the body of a furniture van. It has undergone its last great removal, and sits now, with rear doors open, wheelless, cabless and lifeless. There are several smaller vans, mostly painted powder blue for some reason, an asbestos garage or two, and at least half a dozen retired railway goods vans, no doubt reliving their working past with each train that rattles by.

There is not much chance of anything flowering in these fields: just a few buttercups and a patch or two of nettles. Once a year, for a week or two in May, the weary old hedgerows light up, and hawthorn, blackthorn and damson make a brave attempt to recall the countryside.

I think the reason I enjoy the tattiness of the urban fringe so much, is that it fairly buzzes with activity. From here on the journey becomes so very boring. Nothing but mile after mile of bright green rolling plains. I admit that in the low light of early morning or late evening, the subtle rise and fall of the land can be quite handsome, and in one or two places you can just about make out the light and dark strips where corn is growing over ancient ridge and furrow field patterns. Occasional old stag-headed oaks still stagger on across the open prairies to inconvenience the farmer. They are all that remains of the hedgerow system now, and with so much land drainage and bore-hole pumping to lower the watertable, even their days are definitely numbered. This modern farming landscape does still change with the seasons, of course. The brown earth is hardly ever cultivated now, thanks to direct-drilling and the 'chemical plough' but there is a fresh green flush of germinating seed in March, to mark the end of winter, a blaze of yellow or pink or white as the various oilseed crops come into bloom, and in autumn there is still a

golden season, as the combines crawl through clouds of dust
at harvest-time. Even now, occasional flocks of lapwings can
sometimes be seen, standing stonily against the wind of a
really harsh winter's day, but I can't remember when I last
saw their springtime aerobatics, or watched insect-snapping
swallows racing the shadow of my train across the surface of
the growing corn.

These fields, if you can still call them that, really are huge.
They stretch way beyond the horizon. It is quite a relief to
see the occasional group of buildings, and there is a certain
'majesty' about the steel grey grain silos and the long, low
lines of animal houses, but I still find it odd to think that it
makes better economic sense to cut the grass and take it to
the livestock by tractor, instead of taking the animals to the
grass. 'Zero-grazing' they call it, and it seems to have
completely taken over recently, but I for one miss the sight of
cows and sheep grazing in the fields, and I share the concern
many people have for the way the animals may be suffering
in those anonymous buildings. This kind of farming seems
likely to be as bad for our farm animals as it is for their now
homeless wild cousins.

As the prairie fields get bigger and bigger, and the journey
drags on, I generally find myself nodding off – dreaming of the
way the landscape might be improved. Eventually the pattern
within the prairie begins to change. The first optimistic sign
is a particular group of buildings where the farmer has at least
bothered to plant some trees. Most of them are poplars,
planted to grow quickly, presumably to make up for the
hedgerows he's removed, but also to try and make life on the
prairie a little more comfortable. I've watched this shelterbelt
grow dramatically since it was first planted and although
nothing much in the way of wildlife habitat has ever been able
to survive directly beneath the trees, there is a stretch of
uncultivated land on the windward side, and that has somehow
developed as a bank of thorn scrub. I imagine that must be
quite a popular roost with the sparrows that feed around the
animal-feed hoppers in the yard.

The change of pattern in the fields is subtle at first. You'd
never notice it unless you were a regular traveller like me.
There is just a slight change in the pattern of the colours from
one year to the next. At the moment, for instance, there is
a crop which looks like potatoes just starting to show in neat
stripes across the field on either side of the railway line, but
at this time last year these same fields had a blue-grey haze

over them, which turned out to be the first showings of a crop of broad beans. I can't remember what grew there the year before that, but certainly it was something else again. There is another change that creeps into the prairie soon after the spuds and beans stretch. It reminds me of holidays in the French countryside. The fields are still immense and treeless, but suddenly they become striped. There are great long blocks of distinct colours, and each one is a different crop. There always seems to be a high proportion of grasses, with some cut regularly and presumably fed to animals, whilst other blocks are grown on into panels of wheat or high stands of maize. I can usually spot beans and potatoes again, and quite a few types of pea that I've never seen growing in our veg patch. You sometimes get some startling colour combinations too – I remember a panel of pale blue flowers, linseed I think, growing between a block of yellow rape, and a cornfield that was a sea of poppies. The whole thing was surrounded by the plain green of other crops, and looked for all the world like a giant tricolor.

All this crop rotation is a sure sign that the farmers are beginning to care about the health of their soil again, and the peas and beans help restore fertility for other crops.

I quite often see big birds of prey of one sort or another on this stretch of the journey, either gliding menacingly over the crops, or sitting idly on top of one of the irrigation posts. There will sometimes be a whole crowd of small birds mobbing the predator, swooping and diving to try and drive it away, and just once I actually saw the magnificent sight of a kill. A covey of a dozen or more partridges was quietly pecking away in the rough grass alongside one of the tracks. Just as my railway carriage passed by, a huge bird of prey glided over the edge of an adjacent block of corn, and in a split second it was on the ground, ripping at the carcass of one of the birds. There must be a great many small creatures you cannot possibly spot from the train, to judge by the large number of predators living there. Things have been getting better and better ever since the very high surcharge was placed on pesticides, and farmers were given financial support for employing extra 'husbandry' labour. The combination of the reduced chemical input, and careful crop rotation has surprised everyone by increasing efficiency, dramatically improving the environment, and producing only a minor drop in the size of crop yields. Food surpluses are now at a much more sensible level, and the cost saving on chemical

It may be desperate, but this shows how strong the human urge to live alongside nature is.

imports is helping pay farmers in the less-productive uplands
to manage their farms with a conservation bias.

Wherever there are lower growing vegetable crops between
the blocks of tall corn, there seem to be people working –
hoeing, harvesting, packing the crop into boxes for selling at
the farm gate or shipping off to the local market. The blocks
of flowers are particularly labour-intensive at certain times of
year, but I must say a strip of clarkia, marigolds or tulips
grown for cut flowers does brighten up the landscape. I think
my favourite crop is the sunflowers. I love the way they turn on
their stems. In the morning their big brown faces all smile at
the train, but by late afternoon they've turned their backs
and present a sea of green instead.

When the first crops of sunflowers began to appear they
suffered terribly from summer gales, with whole blocks of
plants smashed to the ground. The shelterbelts are much
further advanced now, though, and there seems no longer
to be a problem. The farms are much less windswept. It is
good to see that some of the blocks of trees are already
needing to be thinned – more jobs for the countryside
workforce.

After travelling through so many shelterbelts, the start of
the real forest always comes as a surprise. You suddenly
realise that the strips of farm crops have stopped, and although
there are still occasional grassy clearings by the railway side,
the whole landscape is dominated by trees. By this time of
year most of the stacks of cut timber have been carted away,
and the freshly coppiced areas are a picture. It is amazing how
the primroses in particular seem to have thrived over the
past few years. This stretch of the journey is especially exciting
if I can manage to catch the early morning train. Whenever I do,
I seem to glimpse one or two fallow deer, nervously browsing
at the edge of the clearings. They seem to have a weakness
for bluebells at this time of year. Usually they glance up at the
passing train, but they never seem terribly bothered by it.
In the winter, when the trees are bare, you can catch glimpses
of footballers running around beyond the forest screen, and
I suspect the deer quite enjoy the blocks of richly fertilised
turf in the various sports clearings through the woodland.
Having plenty of sporting folk around must help make the
woodlands safer for other users too. Certainly there always
seem to be plenty of kids in evidence, and I imagine their
parents just feel the woods are safe for them to play in
because there are always people there to keep an eye out. I

*We have money for short-term
spending, but none for long-term
caring. A house-sized painting of
a snail is no substitute for the real
thing.*

don't seem to see as many forestry workers as you might
expect, but that can only be because you can't see very far
from the train. Their handiwork is obvious, and they must
be working hard to keep the woods in such good trim, but on
the few occasions when I do catch sight of a couple of folk
in hard hats and overalls, they invariably seem to be talking
to kids instead of getting on with more traditional forestry
jobs. I remember once spotting a deeply serious debate
between a forestry official and a couple of young lads. Obviously
I couldn't hear what they were saying, but they were standing
by a pile of branches on the edge of a clearing, and I can only
assume they were discussing the finer points of den
construction. I imagine the foresters must worry a lot about
kids lighting bonfires. It's just as well the workers and the
children seem to understand one another. There is a point a
little further along the line where someone has built a
wonderful tree-house. It is in the branches of an alder which
must be getting close to cropping size and I suspect that, like
me, a lot of my regular fellow-travellers are watching with
interest to see if the foresters will be sensitive enough to leave
it intact, when they come to fell the surrounding crop.

The start of the woodland may creep up on you, but it ends
with startling abruptness. One minute the train is whizzing
along between blurred walls of greenery, and the next we're
in bright sunlight, and slowing down as the railway sets off
across the broad expanse of reedbed and shallow wetlands.
There is a curve in the line at one point, and it is just
possible to see the urban skyline in the distance, completely
dominated by trees. The approaching city rarely gets more
than a glance from me though. The landscape beside the track
is far too compelling. Every year there are more and more
geese on the manmade mudflats, and although most of them
have left by this time of year, returning to the cold north to
breed, there is still plenty of wildlife to be seen. The herons
are a real feature of the journey, standing motionless, often
just a few metres from the foot of the railway embankment,
and there seem to be plenty of waders still, presumably
staking out nesting territory on the grassier bits. I think it was
a stroke of genius on someone's part to schedule a ten
minute stop in the middle of the marsh for every train. No-one
gets on or off, of course, and the birds are so completely
used to the trains that it is possible to see large numbers of
spectacular species at really close quarters. Already there
are one or two families of cleverly camouflaged chicks, and it

is lovely to hear the passengers' comments as they spot a
family of avocets, or a line of black and white shelducklings
trotting in single file behind mum. I quite often see hen
harriers and marsh harriers hunting here, and in the really
cold weather last January there were thousands of duck –
pochard, wigeon, teal and mallard – just sitting looking
miserable, apparently resigned to the fact that the urban
foxes would trot out across the ice each night, and pick off
one or other of the birds for supper. In the late summer,
when the sun sets by about 7.30, there is a period of two or
three days when huge numbers of swallows gather in the
reedbeds, and feed frantically over the marsh and mud before
they up and off to their wintering grounds beyond the
Sahara, and although they are less obvious, these new wetlands
are teeming with dragonflies, frogs, newts and all the other
wild creatures that suffered so much habitat loss in the
seventies and eighties.

It's always a slight disappointment when the engine starts
up again, and the train moves gently on into the city. The
birds seem completely oblivious, but then, apart from the
trains, they rarely have any kind of disturbance. It takes only
three or four minutes from here to reach the central station but
it's a stage of the journey which is packed full of interest.
The energy conservation grants for planting climbers against
buildings have probably made the greatest impact, and the
city really is green now. The private gardens, and the small
gaps in between have all developed as rich shrub-covered
'habitat', and the ban on pesticides has produced a spectacular
increase in butterfly and bird numbers. The 'plague of
locusts' which the chemical manufacturers predicted never
actually materialised of course, and in fact there are rather
fewer pests and disease epidemics in this unpolluted
landscape.

The schools, parks and other municipal landscapes have
become the real high-spots of the city's green network. It is
hard to believe now that they were once such deserts. There
are still small pockets of formal carpet-bedding here and
there, proudly tended by the local allotment societies on a rota
basis, but there are great broad sweeps of colour too, where
yellows and whites decorate the hay meadows, or the more
gaudy 'weeds of cultivation' splash reds, blues and golds
across the mini-cornfields. The overwhelming impression is
that no space is being wasted. Of course there is building
work going on, and each new development means the loss of

some temporary habitat or another, but there are no longer those great expanses of 'development site landscape'. The accountants seem happy now to sow down their investment sites with wildflowers, or flood them as short-life wetlands, and there isn't a house, a factory canteen or an office that doesn't have at least one window overlooking a patch of positively managed wildlife habitat. I must say I'm particularly envious when I see the offices whose lucky managers have windows overlooking the wetland.

In no time at all the journey's over, and I'm concentrating on home. It's only a five minute walk from the station. If it's not too late I often take the slightly longer route through the park: it's so nice to pick a bunch of wildflowers to take home for the table. In any event I'm usually walking up the garden path within a few minutes of leaving the train.

Of course all that is just a dream but I'm most definitely an optimist. Already the signs are there. More and more people are getting angry at the stupid way we treat the environment. Children in particular are beginning to ask my generation just how we can keep on doing such selfish things. With wildlife gardening, tens of thousands of people have begun to 'make a difference'. They've started to do positive things to help the wildlife on their doorstep. Now it is time to become a little braver. You and I have a responsibility to hand on a better, safer, greener world than the one we inherited. If we start now – then maybe the optimistic half of my train journey will become a reality, instead of just a green dream.

There is no shortage of wasted land in towns. At present we spend a great deal of time and money sterilising it. With a bit of imagination, our cities could become the richest kind of 'countryside' imaginable – and that is where I want to live, on the wild side of town.

USEFUL ADDRESSES

NATIONAL VOLUNTARY CONSERVATION ORGANISATIONS

Amateur Entomologists' Society 355 Hounslow Road, Hanworth, Feltham, Middlesex TW13 5JH

Botanical Society of the British Isles c/o Department of Botany, British Museum (Natural History), Cromwell Road, London SW7 5BD; 01-589 6323 ext 701

British Association of Nature Conservationists (BANC), Dept of Geography, University of Lancaster, Bailrigg, Lancaster LA1 4YR; 0524-65201

British Butterfly Conservation Society Tudor House, Quorn, Loughborough, Leics LE12 8AD; 0509-42870

British Trust for Conservation Volunteers (BTCV), 36 St Mary's Street, Wallingford, Oxon OX10 OEU; 0491-39766

British Trust for Ornithology Beech Grove, Tring, Herts HP23 5NR; 044-282 3461

Civic Trust 17 Carlton House Terrace, London SW1; 01-930 0914

Ecological Parks Trust (EPT), c/o The Linnean Society, Burlington House, Piccadilly, London W1V OLQ; 01-734 5170

Fauna and Flora Preservation Society 8–12 Camden High Street, London NW1 OJH; 01-387 9656

Friends of the Earth (FOE), Headquarters, 377 City Road, London EC1V 1NA; 01-837 0731. *Also*

FOE (Scotland) 53 George IV Bridge, Edinburgh EH1 1EJ; 031-225 6906

Henry Doubleday Research Association Ryton on Dunsmore, Coventry CV8 3LG; 0203-303517

Heritage Education Group 17 Carlton House Terrace, London SW1

Interchange City Farms Advisory Service Community Arts and Resource Centre, 15 Wilkin Street, London NW5 3NX; 01-267 9421

Irish Wildlife Federation 112 Grafton Street, Dublin 2, Eire; Dublin (0001) 608346

Keep Britain Tidy Group Bostel House, 37 West Street, Brighton BN1 2RE; 0273-23585

Landlife (formerly Rural Preservation Assoc), The Old Police Station, Lark Lane, Liverpool L17 8UU; 051-728 7011

National Federation of City Farms The Old Vicarage, 66 Fraser Street, Wallingford, Oxon OX10 OEU; 0491-39766. *Also* c/o Hon Secretary, 15 Wilkin Street, London NW5 3NG; 01-267 9421

National Playing Fields Association 25 Ovington Square, London SW3 1LQ; 01-584 6445

Royal Society for Nature Conservation (RSNC), 22 The Green, Nettleham, Lincoln LN2 2NR; 0522-752326

Royal Society for the Protection of Birds (RSPB), The Lodge, Sandy, Beds SG19 2DL; 0767-80551

Think Green Interchange Centre, 15 Wilkin Street, London NW5 3NG

Town and Country Planning Association 17 Carlton House Terrace, London SW1Y 5AS; 01-930 8903/4/5

Wildflower Society Rams Hill House, Horsmonden, Tonbridge, Kent. *Also* 69 Outwoods Road, Loughborough, Leics

Woodland Trust Autumn Park, Dysart Road, Grantham, Lincs NG31 6LL; 0476-74297

World Wildlife Fund UK Panda House, 11–13 Ockford Road, Godalming, Surrey GU7 1OU; 048-68 20551

Young Ornithologists' Club (YOC), The Lodge, Sandy, Beds SG19 2DL

EDUCATION ORGANISATIONS

Council for Environmental Education University of Reading, School of Education, London Road, Reading RG1 5AQ; 0734-875234 ext 218

Council for Urban Studies Centres (CUSC), Streetwork, c/o Notting Dale Urban Studies Centre, 189–191 Feston Road, London W10 6TH; 01-969 8942

Department of Education & Science Elizabeth House, York Road, London SE1 7PH; 01-928 9222

Environmental Education Advisers' Association Pendower Hall Teachers' Centre, West Road, Newcastle upon Tyne NE15 6PP

Epping Forest Conservation Centre High Beach, Loughton, Essex LG10 4AF

Federation of Field Studies Centres Preston Montford Field Centre, Montford Bridge, Shrewsbury, Salop SY4 1DX *Education enquiries; Information Office.*

Glasgow Environmental Education Urban Projects (GEE-UP), Education Offices, 129 Bath Street, Glasgow G2 2SY; 041-204 2900 ext 2639

Horticultural Therapy Training Centre Warwickshire College of Agriculture, Moreton Morrell, Warwickshire CV35 9BL; 0926-651288

National Association for Environment Education Westbourne Teachers' Centre, 17 Westbourne Road, Sheffield S10 2QQ

Slapton Ley Field Centre Slapton, Kingsbridge, Devon TQ7 2QP

Urban Wildlife Group (Education Unit), 11 Albert Street, Birmingham B4 7UA

WATCH (Trust for Environmental Education), 22 The Green, Nettleham, Lincoln LN2 2NR; 0522-752326

ENVIRONMENTAL PROFESSIONAL INSTITUTIONS

Arboricultural Association Administration Section, Ampfield House, Ampfield, Romsey, Hants SO5 9PA; 0794-68717

Association of British Tree Surgeons and Arborists c/o Arboricultural Association, see above

Association of Community Technical Aid Centres (ACTAC), Unit B68B, New Enterprise Workshops, South West Brunswick Dock, Liverpool L3 4AR; 051-708 7607

Association of Playing Field Officers and Landscape Managers 103 Derwent Road, Tettenhall, Wolverhampton WU6 9EU

Association of Professional Foresters Brokerswood House, Brokerswood, Westbury, Wilts BA13 4EH; 0373-822238

British Ecological Society Burlington House, Piccadilly, London W1V OLQ; 01-434 2641

British Effluent and Water Association 51 Castle Street, High Wycombe, Bucks HP13 4RN; 0494-444544

Institute of Archaeology 31–34 Gordon Square, London WC1; 01-387 6052

Institute of Civil Engineers 1/7 Great George Street, Westminster, London SW1P 3AA; 01-222 7722

Institute of Chartered Foresters 22 Walker Street, Edinburgh EH3 7HR; 031-225 2705

Institute of Groundsmanship 19–28 Church Street, Agora, Wolverton, Milton Keynes, Bucks MK12 5LG; 0908-312511

Institute of Leisure and Amenity Management (The parks profession), Lower Basildon, Reading, Berks RG8 9NE; 0491-873558

Institute of Water Pollution Control Ledstone House, 53 London Road, Maidstone, Kent ME16 8JH; 0622-62034

Landscape Institute 12 Carlton House Terrace, London SW1Y 5AH; 01-839 4044

Royal Town Planning Institute 26 Portland Place, London W1N 4BE; 01-636 9107 *Also*

Planning Aid Service for Londoners 01-580 7277

STATUTORY ENVIRONMENTAL INSTITUTIONS

British Railways Board Rail House, Euston Square, London NW1; 01-262 3231

British Waterways Board Melbury House, Melbury Terrace, London NW1 6JX; 01-262 6711

Central Electricity Generating Board 24 Cathedral Place, London EC4P 4EB

Countryside Commission Advisory Services: John Dower House, Crescent Place, Cheltenham, Glos GL50 3RA; 0242-521381

Department of the Environment Central Directorate of Environmental Protection, Room A3.24, DoE, Romney House, 43 Marsham Street, London SW1 3PY; 01-212 5464 *Also* Wildlife Division, Tollgate House, Houlton Street, Bristol, Avon BS2 9DJ; 0272-218811

The Forestry Commission 231 Corstorphine Road, Edinburgh EH12 7AT; 031-334 0303

HM Land Registry 32 Lincoln's Inn Fields, London WC2A 3PH; 01-405 3588

Institute of Terrestrial Ecology Monks Wood, Abbots Ripton, Huntingdon, Cambs; 04873-381

Manpower Services Commission Moorfoot, Sheffield S1 4PQ; 0742-704317

Ministry of Agriculture, Fisheries and Food Whitehall Place, London SW1A 2HH; 01-233 3000

Nature Conservancy Council (NCC), Headquarters & regional office for East Midlands, Northminster House, Northminster Road, Peterborough PE1 1AV; 0733-40345

The Ordnance Survey Ramsey Road, Maybush, Southampton SD9 4DH; 0703-775555

Property Services Agency, DOE 2 Marsham Street, London SW1P 3EB; 01-212 3434

Water Authorities Association 1 Queen Anne's Gate, London SW1H 9BT; 01-222 8111

LOCALLY BASED URBAN WILDLIFE GROUPS

BEDFORD
Beds & Hants Naturalists' Trust 38 Mill Street, Bedford MK40 3HD

BELFAST
Conservation Volunteers Cherryvale Park, Ravenshill Road, Belfast, BT6 OBZ

BIRMINGHAM, WEST BROMWICH, DUDLEY, WOLVERHAMPTON AND WALSALL
Urban Wildlife Group 11 Albert Street, Birmingham B4 7UA

Also **BTCV** Conservation Centre, Firsby Road, Quinton, Birmingham

BRISTOL
Avon Wildlife Trust 209 Redland Road, Bristol BS6 6YU

CARDIFF
BTCV Forest Farm, Forest Farm Road, Whitchurch, Cardiff

COVENTRY
Warwickshire Nature Conservation Trust 1 Northgate Street, Warwick CV34 4SP

DONCASTER
BTCV Training Centre, Balby Road, Balby, Doncaster DH4 0RH

EDINBURGH
Environmental Resource Centre Drummond High School, Cochran Terrace, Edinburgh EH7 4PO

EXETER
Exeter Wildlife Group Garden Flat, 7 Richmond Road, Exeter, Devon EX4 4JA

GATESHEAD
BTCV Springwell Conservation Centre, Springwell Road, Wrekenton, Gateshead, Tyne & Wear NE9 7AD

GLASGOW
Glasgow Urban Wildlife Group 54 Waddel Street, Glasgow G5 0LU

GUILDFORD
Surrey Trust for Nature Conservation Hatchlands, East Clandon, Guildford, Surrey GU4 7RT

LEEDS
Leeds Urban Wildlife Group c/o Dept of Landscape Architecture, Leeds Polytechnic, Brunswick Terrace, Leeds. *Also* **Landlife** 5 Salisbury Street, Rawdon, Leeds LS19 6BE *and* **BTCV**, Hollybush Farm, Broad Lane, Kirkstall, Leeds, Yorks

LEICESTER
City Wildlife Project 31 London Road, Leicester

LINCOLN
Lincoln City Wildlife Survey 4 Eton Close, Hampton Park, Lincoln LN6 0YF

LIVERPOOL
Landlife The Old Police Station, Lark Lane, Liverpool 17

LONDON
London Wildlife Trust (with branches in most London boroughs), 1 Thorpe Close, Notting Hill, London W10 5XL. *Also* **BTCV** 2 Mandela Street, Camden Town, London NW1 *and* **Ecological Parks Trust** c/o Linnean Society, Burlington House, Piccadilly, W1

MACCLESFIELD
Macclesfield Groundwork Trust Brook Bank House, Wellington Road, Bollington, Macclesfield, Cheshire SK10 5JS

MANCHESTER
Impact 39 Northumberland Road, Old Trafford, Manchester M16 9AN
Landlife The Environmental Institute, Greave School, Bolton Road, Swinton, Manchester 27

NEWCASTLE
BTCV Springwell Conservation Centre, Wrekenton, Gateshead, Tyne & Wear NE9 7AD

NORWICH
Norwich Wildlife Group 48 Wellington Road, Norwich NR2 3HT

NOTTINGHAM
BTCV Training Centre, United Reform Church, Gregory Boulevard, Nottingham. *Also* **City Wildlife Group** 42 Green Lane, Lambley, Nottingham *and* **Notts Trust for Nature Conservation** 33 Main Street, Osgathorpe, Loughborough, Leics LE12 9TA

OLDHAM
Groundwork Trust Bank House, 8 Chapel Street, Shaw, Oldham OL2 8AJ

OXFORD
Berkshire, Buckinghamshire, Oxfordshire Naturalists Trust (BBONT) 3 Church Cowley Road, Rosehill, Oxford OX4 3JR

PLYMOUTH
Plymouth Urban Wildlife Group Dept of Natural History, City Museum, Drake Circus, Plymouth PL4 8AJ

PRESTON
BTCV 40 Cannon Street, Preston, Lancs PR1 8NT

RAWTENSTALL
Rossendale Groundwork Trust New Hall Hey Farm, New Hall Hey Road, Rawtenstall, Lancs BB4 6HR

READING
Reading Wildlife Group, BBONT, 39 Liverpool Road, Reading RG1 3PW

ROCHDALE
Groundwork Trust Bank House, 8 Chapel Street, Shaw, Oldham OL2 8AJ

ST HELENS
Operation Groundwork 32/34 Claughton Street, St Helens WA10 1SN. *Also* **Landlife** 26 Kiln Lane, Denton Green, St Helens

SALFORD
Groundwork Trust 6 Kansas Avenue, Weaste, Salford M5 2GL

SHEFFIELD
Sheffield City Wildlife Group 121 Pomona Street, Sheffield S11 8JN

SOUTHAMPTON
Southampton Natural History Society 21 Rownham Road, Maybush, Southampton SO1 6DX

STOCKPORT
Stockport Wildlife Group 10 Brookside Lane, High Lane, Stockport SK6 8HL

STOKE ON TRENT
Staffordshire Trust of Nature Conservation 37 Newport Road, Stafford ST16 2HH. *Also* **New Victoria Theatre** Etruria Road, Newcastle under Lyme, Staffs

SWANSEA
c/o **Lower Swansea Valley Project** Development Dept, Swansea City Council, The Guildhall, Swansea, West Glamorgan SA1 4PH

SWINDON
Wiltshire Trust for Nature Conservation 19 High Street, Devizes, Wilts

TELFORD
Telford Nature Conservation Project Stirchley Grange, Stirchley, Telford, Salop

WIGAN
Groundwork Trust Alder House, Alder Street, Atherton M29 9DT

WORCESTER
Worcestershire Nature Conservation Trust Hanbury Road, Droitwich, Worcs

YORK
Yorkshire Wildlife Trust 20 Castle Gate, York YO1 1RP

USEFUL BOOKS

FIELD GUIDES

BANG, P. and DAHLSTROM, P. *Guide to animal tracks and signs* Collins, rev edn., nd.

BRUNN, P. *'Country Life' Guide to birds of Britain and Europe* Newnes, 2nd rev. edn., 1986.

MACMILLAN *Guide to Britain's nature reserves* Macmillan, 1982.

PHILLIPS, R. *Common and important mushrooms; Garden and field weeds; Native and common trees; Woodland wild flowers* (Photographic natural history guides) Elm Tree, 1986.

Gem nature guides Collins.

Longman nature guides Longman, 1986.

PRACTICAL HANDBOOKS

BAINES, C. and SMART, J. *Guide to habitat creation* G.L.C. 1984. Obtainable from Greater London Ecology Unit, County Hall, London SE1 7B; 01-633 2139.

BAINES, C. *How to make a wildlife garden* Elm Tree, 1985

BECKETT, K. *Planting native trees and shrubs* Jarrold, 1979. op.

BRADSHAW, A. D. and CHADWICK, M. J. *The restoration of land: the ecology and reclamation of derelict and degraded land* Blackwell, 1980.

STREET, M. *Restoration of gravel pits for wildfowl* ARC, 1985. Obtainable from ARC Ltd., The Ridge, Chipping Sodbury, Bristol BS17 6AY; 0454-316000.

WELLS, T., BELL, S. and FROST, A. *Creating attractive grasslands using native plant species* Nature Conservancy Council, nd. Obtainable from NCC, Northminster House, Peterborough PE1 1UA; 0733-40345.

Conservation handbook series British Trust for Conservation Volunteers, nd. Obtainable from BTCV, 36 St. Mary's Street, Wallingford, Oxon OX10 0EU; 0491-39766.

PLANNING AND LAW

DENYER-GREEN, B. *Development and planning law* Estates Gazette, 1982.

LOBBENBERG, S. *Using urban wasteland: a guide for community groups* Bedford Square Press, 1981. op.

WOODWARD, P. and BERGER, R. *Planning with nature: a guide for all who help shape the environment and our towns* (Planners pack) Urban Wildlife Group, 1984. Obtainable from West Midlands Urban Wildlife Trust, 11 Albert Street, Birmingham B4 7UA; 021-236 3626.

see also

The occupiers' and landlords' liability act, 1957 HMSO, 1957.

BOOKS ON URBAN NATURE CONSERVATION

ECOLOGICAL PARKS TRUST *Promoting nature in cities and town* Croom Helm, 1986.

HAMMOND, R. and KING, M. *Nature by design* Urban Wildlife Group, 1984. Obtainable from West Midlands Urban Wildlife Trust.

TEAGLE, W. G. *The endless village: wildlife of Birmingham, Sandwell, Walsall and Wolverhampton* Nature Conservancy Council, 1978.

INDEX